The Social Capitalist

*Passion and Profits
—An Entrepreneurial Journey*

JOSH AND LISA LANNON

The Social Capitalist

*Passion and Profits
—An Entrepreneurial Journey*

JOSH AND LISA LANNON

an imprint of BZK Press

Published by RDA Press
an imprint of BZK Press, LLC

Rich Dad Advisors, B-I Triangle, CASHFLOW Quadrant and other
Rich Dad marks are registered trademarks of CASHFLOW Technologies, Inc.

BZK Press LLC
15170 N. Hayden Road
Scottsdale, AZ 85260
480-998-5400
Visit our Web sites: BZKPress.com and RichDadAdvisors.com

Printed in the United States of America

First Edition: November 2012

ISBN: 978-1-937832-08-7

Dedication

We dedicate this book to those that have lost their lives,
or their loved ones, to addiction.
And to those committed to creating change for
themselves and the lives of others.

A portion of the proceeds from this book will be donated
to **Free the Children** www.freethechildren.com, the
charity partner of **Me to We** www.metowe.com

Free the Children – is an International charity and
educational partner, working to enable youths to be
agents of change.

Me to We – is an innovative social enterprise that offers
socially conscious and environmentally friendly products
and life-changing experiences.

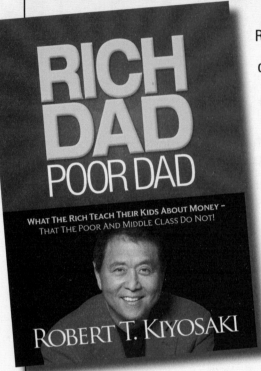

Best-Selling Books
In the Rich Dad Advisors Series

by Blair Singer

SalesDogs
You Don't Have to Be an Attack Dog to Explode Your Income

Team Code of Honor
The Secrets of Champions in Business and in Life

by Garrett Sutton, Esq.

Start Your Own Corporation
Why the Rich Own their Own Companies and Everyone Else Works for Them

Writing Winning Business Plans
*How to Prepare a Business Plan that Investors will Want to Read –
and Invest In*

Buying and Selling a Business
How You Can Win in the Business Quadrant

The ABCs of Getting Out of Debt
Turn Bad Debt into Good Debt and Bad Credit into Good Credit

Run Your Own Corporation
*How to Legally Operate and Properly Maintain Your Company
into the Future*

The Loopholes of Real Estate
Secrets of Successful Real Estate Investing

by Ken McElroy

The ABCs of Real Estate Investing
The Secrets of Finding Hidden Profits Most Investors Miss

The ABCs of Property Management
What You Need to Know to Maximize Your Money Now

The Advanced Guide to Real Estate Investing
How to Identify the Hottest Markets and Secure the Best Deals

by Tom Wheelwright

Tax-Free Wealth
How to Build Massive Wealth by Permanently Lowering Your Taxes

by Andy Tanner

Stock Market Cash Flow
Four Pillars of Investing for Thriving in Today's Markets

by Josh and Lisa Lannon

The Social Capitalist
Passion and Profits
—An Entrepreneurial Journey

Acknowledgments

This book would not have been possible without the dedication and commitment from our incredible team at Journey Healing Centers.

To our families, who have loved us through the years, even when they didn't understand or agree with our choices, both during the hard times and even today.

And to our mentors and teachers: Robert and Kim Kiyosaki, Mr. Paul Mills, Chris Spencer, Blair Singer, Kelly Ritchie, and those leading all the different personal development training workshops and seminars we have participated in over the years.

Thank you to Garrett Sutton for your legal advice and your contribution to this book, to Kathy Heasley, Jessica Santina and Mona Gambetta for their editing on the manuscript.

Thank you to Jon Carson, Bill Drayton, Christopher "Kreece" Fuchs, F. Xavier Helgesen, R. Christine Hershey, Michael Holthouse, Rommel Juan, Liz Maw Bruce McNamer, David Murphy, Jess Sand, Mirjam Schöning, and Julie Smolyansky for the information and expertise that you provided and your valuable time.

And thank *you,* for having the strength to take a stand.

Contents

Foreword
by Robert Kiyosaki

I am very proud of Josh and Lisa.

Many people believe that I write my books and create my educational games just to teach people to make money or simply to earn money. That is only partially true.

While I am happy that people are attaining a bit more financial security, especially in these challenging economic times, I am more appreciative of people who are doing what Josh and Lisa have done. What they have done is become social capitalists.

I believe that each of us has a special and unique gift to give, and Lisa and Josh are giving their gift. They've confronted the challenges that life has put in their path and battled adversity. They've found strength in each other and in what they, together, have created.

Today they are going well, financially and spiritually, by doing good in our world.

They saw a need within our society and created a business to serve that need.

They applied sound business and investing principles in growing their business and today have accomplished several things. They have addressed a need in our world, become real estate investors, built a business that supports them and their family—as well as the families of their employees around the world. They lead by example within their communities and as parents to their young children.

If you believe you have a special gift to give, or just want to make the world a better place by being an entrepreneur, this book is for you. You, too, can be a Social Capitalist.

– Robert Kiyosaki

Introduction

"Never doubt that a small group of thoughtful, committed citizens can change the world. Indeed, it is the only thing that ever has."

—Margaret Mead

On November 26, 2001, I was well on my way to becoming one of the 79,000 people that the Centers for Disease Control and Prevention say die each year from excessive alcohol use. I had come home that morning after a three-day bender, my depression and insecurity a raging inferno fueled by alcohol, and found myself staring down the barrel of my AR-15 Bushmaster 223 assault rifle, contemplating how much of my wife Lisa's misery and mine I could end by firing the gun.

Shame over what that would do to Lisa, a Las Vegas Metro law enforcement officer who had been cleaning up my messes for years and who would be returning any moment from her 12-hour shift, kept me from pulling the trigger that day. But, ironically, it was the hallucinations that had plagued and terrified me for months that ultimately saved my life. Because on that morning, a vision came to me and whispered the words that changed my life forever: "No ... Not yet. There's more work to do."

Over the course of the next year, I began that work. When Lisa gave me an ultimatum between our marriage or my addiction, I entered drug rehab and sobered up, broke away from my family business and a lifestyle that were killing me, discovered my life's passion, became a father, and laid the groundwork on the first Journey Healing Center (JHC), one of six addiction recovery and rehabilitation healing centers that Lisa and I founded.

When we formed the idea for JHC, we had two goals in mind: No matter what, I must stay sober, and we would, together, build a *sustainable* business. What occurred over the course of that year – the lessons we learned, the decisions we made, the steps we took that enabled Lisa and me to make the jump from being an officer and a nightclub general manager to owners of a socially conscious business that has given us both financial freedom and a deep sense of personal satisfaction – is the foundation of this book.

The words "sustainable business" are particularly important here, and were the distinctive guiding principle behind the writing of these pages. Because back in early 2002, we had no idea that what we were planning would make us part of a growing tidal wave, a surge of private enterprises focused on bettering the world that had begun to be coined "social entrepreneurship," "conscious capitalism" and "social capitalism."

A tidal wave it absolutely has been. Over the last decade, social entrepreneurship has grown exponentially, due to a number of factors. First, funding and resources for this particular brand of entrepreneurship have sprung up, providing greater opportunities where before there were few besides banks. Second, faith in Corporate America at large, and in its concern for our well-being in particular, have diminished. And third, social entrepreneurs' labors can be seen bearing real fruit in terms of both doing good for the world and creating real wealth.

No longer are aspirations to saving the world relegated to the non-profit realm. In 2004, *Fast Company* created its Social Capitalist Awards, which honor those who use their business acumen to solve social problems. In 2010, the term "conscious capitalism" gained huge traction when it became the subject of *Megatrends 2010*, the third in the bestselling Megatrends series. In 2011, three of *Inc. Magazine*'s "30 Under 30" top entrepreneurs were engaged in social enterprises. And today, there are seven states that have adopted the Benefit Corporation status, a new, specially designated business entity intended to distinguish social enterprises from other businesses and non-profit organizations.

As the global economy continues to limp along, legions of downsized and disillusioned workers around the world are making their opportunities while making the world a better place, which is why the term "social entrepreneurship" seems to be a trendy new concept. But the truth is, it's not new. As you'll discover in the pages to come, social entrepreneurs were hard at work bringing their passions to life long before there was a name for what they did.

But what we set out to do when we started Journey Healing Centers was to serve others by working to treat substance abuse, and to build personal wealth by applying the *Rich Dad* principles to our lives. Social entrepreneurs have, traditionally, focused on providing products or services to the poor and under-privileged. In our experience treating addiction, we know that social problems aren't the exclusive domain of the poor or under-privileged; they exist in *all* socioeconomic classes, in all races and ethnicities and age groups. We raised the capital, created new jobs, designed a business that made sense, grew a healthy bottom line, and assisted people in the process. We are Social Capitalists.

Social Capitalists have the strength to face problems that send others running. We know that the government can't solve all our problems. We know that they can't give our power away by becoming dependent on governments and large corporations for our well-being. We take charge of our own lives, and create our own solutions while creating a path for financial security, putting ourselves and others the fast track toward financial freedom.

And since you've picked up this book, we suspect that there may be a Social Capitalist lurking inside you, too. If you've ever thought that you might have it in you to start a business, wondered why you never felt fulfilled working for other people, asked whether there was a way to turn your passion into a profitable enterprise, wanted to add a socially conscious component to your existing business, or wanted to know how to leverage a solution you've found to an existing problem, this book is for you.

In the following chapters, we'll share the story of how we went from being financially ignorant employees to financially savvy business owners and investors on the fast track, and we'll share a few of our secrets, and the secrets of other Social Capitalists, for building a business around the heart – a business that's financeable, leverageable, expandable, and predictable.

We'll provide you with a blueprint for becoming a Social Capitalist, highlight the new uses of the Benefit Corp, and reveal to you how a passion-driven business can have a triple-bottom line, delivering **profit, social value, and freedom**.

As you read this book, you will find parts of the story being told from Josh's point of view or in first person as he is telling it and in the third person or being told from the collective "we" perspective. We chose to write this way to make it easy for you, the reader, to read. However this is both our stories, as we walked the path together, learned together, built and grew the business together, went through the good, bad, ugly and great together and have committed to this journey together. A lot of Lisa's story and perspectives is included in the "we" portion of the book and in the "I" (Josh's voice) portion. Lisa's input is also included in sidebars or textboxes throughout the book.

The 5 Points of Social Capitalism

If you're looking for a book on the steps involved in starting a business, there are plenty of sources better, more interesting, and definitely more knowledgeable than either of us. Any of the books in the *Rich Dad Advisor Series* can provide you with valuable information on anything from writing business plans to strengthening your sales force, motivating a team, understanding taxes, forming a corporation, or growing profits.

You'll find that the *Rich Dad* and Rich Dad Advisor principles will apply to any business. Our focus here is exclusively on Social Capitalism, and harnessing your desire to contribute to the world in a meaningful way while satisfying your hunger for personal fulfillment and a rich life, in every sense of the word.

We've broken this idea into five salient points:

1. **Understanding the tenets of Social Capitalism:** Many entrepreneurs, particularly social entrepreneurs, take a position of poverty. We were led to believe that in order to do God's, or humankind's, work, means taking a vow of poverty. But if you look at many of today's Social Capitalists – Tom's Shoes, Annie's Homegrown, Inc., Odwalla, and even Starbucks – it's obvious that Social Capitalists don't have to be poor, and we'll show you why.

2. **When the student is ready, the teacher appears:** God, the universe, Buddha, life, fate ... whatever you want to call it ... is always ready to teach us, when we're ready to listen. For years, I struggled with addiction that kept me from recognizing the teachers that had important lessons to share with me. When I finally shed the anger, fear, and addiction, and when Lisa and I, together, opened our eyes, the teachers began revealing themselves to us in amazing ways. We'll show you how there are no accidents; your past is one of your greatest assets, and mentors come into our lives when they're supposed to. After all, you've picked up this book. Something is calling you to serve a higher purpose, to play a bigger game in life.

3. **Finding your "why":** You can't, and shouldn't, build a socially conscious business unless you are passionate about the cause. If your business is going to work, it absolutely *must* be built around what's in your heart. For us, this meant addressing addiction. Fighting this monster that had taken so much from us was the force that drove us every single day, through good and bad times – and there were plenty of bad times. What keeps you going through good and bad? What's your "why" for forming a business? What will keep you going each and every day, wanting to work and give it your all? So many business owners have profitable, successful businesses that don't fulfill them. Spiritually or emotionally, they're dying inside – they aren't fulfilled, because they aren't truly passionate about their businesses and their outcomes. We'll show you how to find your own "why," and how you can turn that into a new business, or tap into that "why" to bring a fulfilling social component into your work or existing business.

4. **The Fight:** Lisa and I were both born into alcoholism. I was an addict myself, and Lisa worked in law enforcement, wrestling with substance abuse, which was the root cause of much of the crime she fought on a day-to-day basis. We were both born to fight addiction. For us to have started a social enterprise

that feeds the hungry is a worthy goal, but it wasn't our fight. It wasn't the "why" that got us out of bed each day, ready to fight. What's your fight? What is it that you *must* take on? We'll show you how we recognized our fight, and how you'll know yours, too.

5. **The Global Social Capitalist Movement:** As the Social Capitalist movement continues to gain traction around the world, social entrepreneurs continue to cite finances as their primary obstacle. Your typical bank, angel investor, or venture capitalist may not immediately see the payoff in social enterprise, which makes finding funding through traditional sources difficult. We'll show you how funding Social Capitalism is unique, where there are resources to support your goal, how a unique corporate entity called the Benefit Corp works to protect Social Capitalists, and how to leverage the capital you receive.

We want to thank you for picking up this book, and for being willing to consider a life of service to the world we live in. And we congratulate you for daring to dream of a life different from your current one, a life in which you may face obstacles, and which may force you to question all your beliefs.

We're sharing our story with you to show you that through all our hard work, and through all the challenges we overcame and the lessons we learned, we are rewarded every day, not just financially, but emotionally and spiritually as well. Knowing we've contributed to improving the lives of thousands of people affected by substance abuse is, in itself, unbelievably rewarding. Knowing that, if we stay on track, our financial freedom will enable us to continue doing this for the rest of our lives makes that reward even sweeter.

So if you're ready to turn *your* passion into profits, let's get started!

Chapter One

Our Story

"Neo, sooner or later you're going to realize, just as I did, that there's a difference between knowing the path and walking the path."

—Morpheus, *The Matrix,* 1999

Josh's Story

In 1999, Lisa and I saw the movie *The Matrix*. It's the story of Neo, a computer programmer, who learns that the world he lives in is nothing but an illusion created by computers to subdue people. Throughout the course of the movie, he fights, with the help of others, to free himself from this web of deceit, called "The Matrix," and live free in a true reality.

Science fiction isn't really our thing, but for some reason the film haunted us. It had nothing to do with its elaborately choreographed fight scenes and cutting-edge special effects. It was that Lisa and I had each been brought up feeling as if our lives were predetermined, or programmed for us, and we'd both always felt frustrated by the pressure to conform. We just couldn't shake the feeling that we were, in a sense, in our own matrix, and both of us felt the urge to break free.

I had been that kid in class who maddeningly questioned everything my teacher (and my parents, for that matter) said. Never content with simply doing what I was told and accepting the boundaries set for me, I drove teachers so nuts that after a while, they'd eventually look at me and say, "Please, just be quiet and do your work, okay?"

It was a kind of torture for me to sit in school for hours, and that played out in my grades, which were usually low, if not failing. I felt like I was outside with my face pressed up against the window, but no matter how hard I knocked or yelled, no one noticed me, so I never could join their conversation.

At the schools I attended in Southern California, I began to develop a reputation among teachers, who described me with words like "disruptive," "doesn't apply himself," and even "learning disability." My parents heard these words and took me to medical professionals, who put me on medication that would help me to calm down and "focus."

I became convinced at an early age that I just wasn't cut out for school, and since I already felt like I didn't fit in, I embraced it, became almost proud of it. If they didn't want me to fit in, then I didn't need them. I did whatever I could *not* to fit in. I skipped a lot of school, was referred to by the A students as "a slacker" and "a stoner," and eventually just quit school altogether. If putting in twelve years of school, attending four years of college, and getting a "good job" were their formula for success, then, I figured, I just wouldn't be successful.

But I had come from a family of nightclub owners, so I had access to another world – a world I had often overheard the adults talking about, and which my classmates had never seen. At age 11, I had my first drink, and finally, *finally,* I felt like I fit in. In this world, there were people like me, people in pain, people who had been unfairly labeled, people who didn't fit the mold. In this world, we'd found a way to deaden that pain and eliminate our stress. While this world felt comforting and familiar to me, it was also somehow thrilling. And since it had been good enough for my father, I believed that it was meant for me, too.

My dad, who has, to date, owned a total of fourteen nightclubs in California, Hawaii, and Las Vegas, hired me when I was 19 as a bar back at Dylan's Dance Hall and Saloon in Vegas, where I stocked the bar with liquor, ice, and supplies. It was a menial job, but I absorbed every bit of information I could. I worked hard and became the master of my work. I took pride in keeping the bars fully stocked and delivering three cases of beer at a time, zig-zagging though the crowded nightclub. I knew that if I did a good job, I could work my way up to bartender, make good money, and attract the older girls who came to drink there. Playing in that adult underworld, I felt like I could win in *this* world.

Lisa's Story

Although Josh had never done what he was told to do as a kid, I, for the most part had. My mother was from Vietnam, and had married my dad who was an American soldier there during the Vietnam War. After his tour of duty, my mom left her homeland, her culture, her family and friends to begin life with my dad, who became a deputy sheriff in South Dakota, so that one day my brother and I would have a better life. For her, this American Dream was synonymous with a good education and job security, the kind that led to a good, stable salary and a retirement package.

My mother had grown up in a country that didn't offer the same opportunities as we have in the U.S., and who therefore pushed me to have the life that she herself had never had. I did just as I was expected – I earned good grades in school and enrolled in a journalism program in college, all the while wondering what else was out there.

When I was a young girl, I went out to run errands with my mother one day. I was always curious about buildings and certain one's in town always caught my attention. I pointed to an office building with beautiful architecture. "Whose building is that?" I asked.

"I don't know, rich people's," my mother said.

This only led to more questions from me: "Who are the rich people? How did they get that building? How can we be rich and get a building, too?"

Although I didn't yet know how, I intuitively knew that I would travel the world and have money some day. So I questioned my mother's beliefs about success because, from my early experience, I also knew that my family didn't have what most rich people had. While I had a pretty good upbringing, lots of friends and was happy, I knew there was a bigger world out there. Success, I had already began to see, was elusive and tenuous. I watched my parents work hard for very little reward; we weren't able to do a lot of extra's that cost additional money. Money was tight and they couldn't seem to get out of the cycle of working paycheck to paycheck. According to my parents, college was the way out of that cycle, at least until I found a different answer, so that was the path I took.

With two years of college under my belt and $300 in my pocket, I left my small town home in South Dakota, determined to taste some freedom of my own. I wanted to see something new and exciting – for my best friend and me that meant Las Vegas. With no job or any sort of a plan, I enrolled at UNLV, put a deposit and first months rent down on an apartment and moved the big city. It took a couple months before I got my first job at the Children's Museum. I had run out of money, had borrowed from a friend to pay rent and was starting to worry when this position came along. It was a great first learning experience (although I probably didn't say great at the time) in dealing with the emotional roller coaster of money. A few months later I got a second job at a local bank.

And as "good girls" from South Dakota do, I also partied hard. Nearly every evening, I went out drinking with my girlfriends. On one such Friday night in December 1993, I walked into Dylan's, where Josh had begun working as a bar back, and boy he was mesmerized (that's a story for some other time!). We didn't actually meet until 1995 (he had been sending me free drinks for 1.5 years), but we fell deeply in love very quickly, and five years later, we were married.

The Vacuum
Josh's Story

Las Vegas is the world's largest vacuum. Time doesn't exist there – just look at any casino and you'll be hard-pressed to find a window or a clock. That town sucks up everything in its wake, including your sense of personal responsibility, your decorum, any financial control, or your ability to keep your urges in check. It's where you go to lose yourself, your money, or anything that's important to you. That's why "what happens in Vegas stays in Vegas."

You can't become a responsible adult when you grow up in that environment. Well, at least I certainly couldn't.

At Dylan's, my job included filling the house with thirsty customers, controlling inventory, ensuring our customers had the best possible experience, keeping the cash registers ringing, and, most importantly, guarding the cash. It was why I had a handgun, and it was why I continued studying martial arts. I had begun to be a martial athlete at age 17 when I had lived in Kona, Hawaii. I had studied the kickboxing and ground fighting discipline known as Paul Mills American Kenpo Karate.

Most 21-year-olds think they're unstoppable, but the power I wielded as a gun-owning, martial arts-trained bartender and part nightclub-owner in Vegas convinced me that I was absolutely invincible. And maybe I was just plain crazy, which is pretty common in Las Vegas. An opportunity presented itself, and I opened my own nightclub, called JD's, in the old Calamity Jane's building on Fremont Street, complete with live bands and mosh pits that required almost nightly visits from the police. All the while, I was drinking and partying with the customers, matching shot for shot, spending my money on ridiculous toys, going on all-night runs, and telling myself, "I could do this forever," as I convinced myself that I was the one person who had found all the keys to a perfect life.

Within a year's time, I had run the club into the ground and had put my future, my health, and my relationship with Lisa in jeopardy.

For Lisa, life with me was a constant adrenaline rush, and like with anything else, adrenaline is great in small doses, but eventually it wears you out. She lived with steady, high doses of adrenaline, she began to lose her taste for the partying, and she could see that I was spinning out of control.

It was a tough position for her to be in, considering that not long after we began dating, I began training her to bartend at Dylan's. She was a witness firsthand to the dangers of intoxication, with both drinking and with the nightclub, partying lifestyle. A few years into it, she decided that this life wasn't really for her. She decided to follow in her father's footsteps instead, and took the tests necessary to become a commissioned law enforcement officer for the Las Vegas Metropolitan Police Department. She had joined the force out of her desire to find exciting work, but also to do work that inspired her and contributed to bettering the world in some way. She has always been a protector at heart, and this field suited her much more than slinging drinks and getting drunk.

She found all that, but she was also surprised to find that being in law enforcement, in itself, was an existence that was a little too stable for her liking. After all, Lisa was also exposed to the easy-cash, VIP-treatment lifestyle. Her fellow officers would talk about "putting in their twenty years" and making their career million. And Lisa's first thought was, "Twenty years to make a million dollars? A million for your entire career? Will a million dollars even be a lot of money in twenty years? Some people make a million dollars in a month!" While that was great money for law enforcement, it was not what she wanted to do for the next 20 years to earn it.

Like I said, she and I both see the world very differently from most people. Intuitively, even as she was establishing a good career as an officer, and enjoyed the work, the mission, and the power of her badge. But Lisa also knew that there was something else out there that suited her better. There had to be. Until then, this would do for the short term.

On a nightly basis, Lisa's job in law enforcement meant anticipating the unexpected. She never knew who she was going to wind up interacting with each night, how they would act, or what bizarre situations they might be part of. Many of them were addicts, and many of them unpredictable and often dangerous. Then, she'd come home after a shift to face even worse: her own husband, fresh

I feel it's important to state that many are happy working a career they love and the money that goes with it. But also to look at your dreams and long term goals and ask yourself if the current situation you are in is the means or way you will get there. You can then re-evaluate what your next steps are on accomplishing your dream, is it being an employee, self-employed, business owner or investor and what do you get to do or change to get there. As mentioned in the Introduction, the sidebars are Lisa's additional input throughout the book.

off a three-day run, hungover, hating himself, and pissed off at the world. Her worry was her constant companion; she expected that any day, she'd get the call reporting that I was dead or injured, or that I might end up in jail with her "customers."

Instead of that keeping me on the straight and narrow, it actually had the opposite effect. I hated myself for what I was doing to Lisa, and that self-hatred caused me, ironically, to drown my sorrows in booze, to party even harder to silence the noise in my head. I'd grown up in a stereotypically Irish family of alcoholics, and this is all I knew of coping with pain; people in pain drank.

So I kept drinking, and Lisa, too afraid to start the fight that would inevitably happen if she confronted me about drinking, said nothing. She knew that fighting with me would accomplish nothing: It wouldn't stop me from going out, and it would ultimately only make us both feel worse.

This wasn't the strong, independent Lisa I had married, the one who had struck out on her own, moved to Las Vegas from South Dakota to start a new life and had become an officer. That Lisa spoke her mind, but this Lisa had lost her voice with me. She felt responsible for my addiction by continuing to enable it, not wanting to deal with it, and sad that our relationship seemed to be eroding by the day. The only thing that kept her with me was that, on rare occasions, she saw glimmers of the innocent, ambitious 20-year-old she'd fallen in love with.

Plus, part of her blamed herself. She wondered if she should have seen my addiction coming, or if she had enabled it. After all, I had trained her to bartend, too, and she'd spent plenty of time at the clubs with me. Wasn't she supporting that lifestyle, even being rewarded for it? As a child, she'd watched her parents and grandparents drinking beer and cocktails, eventually getting louder and bawdier as the nights wore on. In her experience, alcohol made things fun. It had made our time together fun, too. Working together in the early part of our relationship, she reasoned, had kept us close, but could it now be tearing us apart?

The fact that we were flush with cash seemed, at the time, like a sign that we were making all the right moves. In retrospect, it only exacerbated the problems we were having as a couple. We'd leave the bar with a wad of cash every night, and as fast it came in, we spent it on racy cars, lavish dinners at expensive Vegas restaurants, and wild nights at the swankiest clubs. We felt like high rollers, tipping $50 and $100 bills like they were Monopoly money. The feeling that we were royalty was very seductive. The joy of being carefree overshadowed any doubts we had about our lifestyle. We lived for many years in the bliss that only comes with ignorance.

But we were anything but free. I was, in fact, completely trapped by the choices I'd made, and the environment we were in. I was undoubtedly in the trap of addiction. But we were also trapped by our lifestyle; we'd created such a luxurious lifestyle for ourselves that we now felt as if we had no choice but to keep doing what we were doing.

It was about this time that we saw *The Matrix* and drove home, silent, each of us thinking about Neo (but too afraid to admit it out loud), "That's exactly how I feel. I'm trapped in a life I don't want."

The Bottom

Our lives continued this way for years, as we hid behind our jobs, our money, and our belongings in order to avoid the real problem staring us in the face: my addiction. By late 2001, I had blown through nearly all of the money we had convinced ourselves we were rolling in, and I had begun stealing money from the nightclub just to maintain the addiction. I had skipped out on many of my responsibilities at home and at work, even avoiding work by frequently calling in sick or just disappearing altogether. I had lost a substantial amount of weight, since the only thing I seemed to be ingesting these days was alcohol; I was unable to hide my malnourishment. And Lisa and I were beginning to drift apart, because the only thing I seemed to care about anymore was my next run.

The subject of my heavy drinking and partying had come up numerous times in our conversations, and I had committed, for Lisa, to attempting more restraint. *It's not like I'm an alcoholic*, I thought. *Alcoholics can't stop drinking. If I really wanted to, I could stop for a week at a time; an alcoholic can't do that.* I just liked going out and partying, having fun with my friends. We were just doing shots, relieving the pressures of work and toasting good times. There was nothing wrong with that, was there?

So sure, I'd work to control the drinking, I said. I would just cut back on the number of drinks I had on a daily basis. I created workarounds, rules that would curb my behavior but still allow me to drink. They included rules like, "I'll only drink after work," or, my personal favorite, "I'll only drink beer." But as anyone whose life has been touched by addiction knows, that was pure delusion.

On November 23, 2001, Lisa and I went out with our friends, Chris, a fellow police officer, and his wife, Jen, to dinner at the Tiller Man Restaurant. In preparation for this night out, I had avoided taking even so much as a sip of alcohol that whole week, and I was feeling it. "What do you think about having a drink with dinner?" I asked Lisa, nearly bursting out of my skin with anticipation.

Setting boundaries and sticking to them is a key component in dealing with a loved one who is in an addiction cycle. I had set boundaries but wasn't always good at sticking to them. I loved Josh and would ultimately let him have his way because I was afraid of what would happen if I didn't.

She debated for a few seconds, looking at me as if scanning to see if I was too anxious. I gave her my best poker face. She clearly wasn't happy about it; her eyes plainly said "no," but I'd put her on the spot and she couldn't argue. She remained silent, faking a smile to me through clenched teeth.

I kissed her on the cheek and quickly summoned a server to bring me a double Stoli and cranberry on the rocks.

Three minutes later, feeling good and enjoying an evening out with friends, I thought nothing of ordering another round when our server reappeared to check on us. It didn't even dawn on me what I'd done until I noticed Lisa glaring at me, her eyes full of disappointment. I'd put her in a frustrating situation – she couldn't even say anything, for fear of embarrassing me in front of our friends. Instead, she withdrew more, already consumed with anger and dread over the inevitable binge of self-destruction that I had just set in motion. And because she was scheduled to work the night shift at the jail for the next three nights, this dinner had all the makings of the perfect storm.

As the night wore on, my plan hatched. I pulled Chris aside to ask if he was up for a night out with me after dinner. He was. After we all said our goodbyes, Chris and I dropped our wives off at home. I gave Lisa a feeble excuse, something about "checking in on business," which she saw through immediately but said nothing. I gave her a quick kiss goodbye, and assured her I'd be home soon, which we both knew was a lie.

Lisa looked at me, clearly seething with anger at me and, perhaps, at her own complete lack of control of the situation. But that was also tempered with fear. She never knew anymore whether she'd be seeing me for the last time. All she could say was, "Okay. I love you, Josh."

I kissed her quickly, avoiding her eyes as I strapped on my Glock 45-caliber handgun and grabbed a wad of cash from our safe, and muttered, "Love you too."

I opened the door and heard, on my way out, "Be safe. Come home soon." I left for The Library, a topless bar owned by my father, to meet Chris and get the party started.

There wasn't much I could say. I would be going to work soon and knew he would leave the house anyways. It was a cycle that happened over and over throughout the years to where we were just going through the motions. It was a no-win situation. I felt like I had lost a part of who I was during this time and I was done.

Lisa spent the next three days upset and increasingly resolute. This certainly wasn't the first time she'd seen me pull this kind of stunt, disappearing for days, but this time, for some reason, it felt different. This time, she was convinced, would be the last. Because even if I made it home alive, Lisa was determined to end the madness. Her resolve grew stronger with every passing day: If I wouldn't agree to get some professional help for my drinking, she was prepared to leave me.

Meanwhile, Chris didn't stay at The Library with me but a couple of hours. Responsible to the core and loyal to my family, he was sure to ask me what my plans were – was I headed home, too? I told him I would be, just so that if Lisa asked him about me, he could report honestly that I'd been planning to return home soon. I knew that if Lisa really wanted to find me, she would. She was a natural detective, and she knew all my favorite haunts.

I spent the next 24 hours hitting several casinos, eventually growing bored enough to call a few party friends and make a plan to meet up at Cheetahs, and then Crazy Horse 2, both strip clubs, both perfect places to disappear with my friends and drink. Now don't get the wrong idea here, strip clubs aren't that glamorous, and our wives had been there many times with us. I was buying, so it was a hard offer for my friends to refuse, and none did. By November 26 – day three of my run – I was a complete mess and it was finally time to crawl home.

I had timed it just so that when I arrived in the middle of the night, Lisa would have left for work already, and she wouldn't have to see me like this – beaten up, depressed, broke, and reeking of alcohol and strip clubs.

I had convinced myself that carrying a handgun was a matter of necessity; it was essential, in my line of work, and in a city this tough, to protect myself. But if I'm being honest, I was terrified of the hallucinations that plagued me every time I drank or took drugs. They took the form of dark, haunting shadows moving around the room and around me, paralyzing me with fear. Wearing the gun gave me an irrational sense of comfort.

But as I entered our home and crawled onto our couch, confronted with depression and loneliness as real as our furniture, as well as a troubled sense that I'd done irreparable damage to Lisa and our marriage, that gun gave me comfort in a new way. It offered a way out. I was my own enemy, I knew that, and here, face to face with my enemy and with no one to stop me, my way became clear. I had struggled for years with the temptation of suicide, and on this night, I thought, maybe the madness could finally end. I began to sob from utter despair, now believing there was nothing I could do to improve this situation but end my own life.

Over the course of the weekend, I had grown stronger in my resolution that I was done. I didn't want to lose Josh but I could no longer go on feeling the way I did. I wanted to be happy again, and those days were few and far between. It felt like the only time I was happy was at work and I was tired of the worrying about Josh and whether he would end up dead, in the hospital or in jail.

My next memory is of sitting on the couch with my Bushmaster 223 AR-15 assault rifle in a sort of trance, resigned to ending my life as quickly and efficiently as possible. I had spent over an hour cleaning, oiling, and reassembling the firearm. It was my process of honoring the weapon and preparing for death—the Samurai's "way of the warrior," or *bushido*. Yet I was ashamed of what I had become.

Hallucinatory shadows darted around me, clambering around the house, making ominous sounds and whispering terrible things to me. I took my weapon in my hands, sprang from the couch, and began walking the house, breathing heavily, clearing it room by room, and pointing the muzzle of the barrel into the darkness. My martial arts training was kicking in, and I was going through the motions, but what I was chasing, I still don't know.

Why am I doing this? I asked myself, looking down in confusion at the rifle in my hands. *What am I doing? There's no one here.* I then began thinking about turning the gun on myself. *Am I really about to shoot myself with my rifle, in our home, so that Lisa can find me?*

Lisa had been cleaning up my messes for years. Did I really think that killing myself this way, so that she could find me in a bloody mess on our floor, was going to *help* her?

I was so disgusted with myself, and full of fear. The hallucinations taunted me again, and I screamed a terrified, "Aaaahhh!"

The full force of what I'd planned to do hit me like a sucker punch. I dropped to the floor, letting go of the rifle, and cried so hard I couldn't breathe. *Can't I kill myself the right way?* I wondered. Could I do anything right?

After a long time spent crying on the floor of the hall, an idea occurred to me like another sick voice in my head. My martial arts training was so refined that I could do it myself, through autonomic control. I could meditate deeply with extreme focus, which I had done many times before. But this time, if I could meditate deeply enough to block out physical pain and tap into energy, I could also reverse the process and shut down my body, depleting it of energy using those same methods. This last, deep meditation would just go deeper than I'd gone before. There would be no blood, no mess to clean up. Clean and efficient. This was my way out.

I crawled on my hands and

I don't know how we had gotten to this point, how we let our lives spin this far out of control, it wasn't supposed to be like this. I knew my decision could go one of two ways and although I didn't want to lose Josh, I knew that was a possibility. Addiction would eventually kill him and I was always torn on how would I feel if it happened after I left him, would I feel like it was my fault because I didn't stay? Was there something I could do? How would I feel if I stayed and he died? I knew that by giving him a choice it would allow me to move forward and not feel the burden of that weight. I hadn't talked to him all weekend so I had no idea the shape he was in, or what he was thinking, I just knew that we both were hurting.

knees into our home office, then lay down, preparing myself to enter the meditation that would ultimately shut down my body. I focused on pulling the energy from my feet and hands through my limbs and up into my body, then dropping that life force back to earth. I repeated this, pulling and pulling energy through my body and then down to the ground. I focused on my breathing and could feel the frigid cold in each part of my body as it slowly, limb by limb, became lifeless.

When I could no longer feel or move my limbs, I then focused on my head and neck, pulling the energy into my chest and into the ground. I pulled deeper and deeper into the darkness. I grew colder and colder, and finally I could no longer feel my body. Then I blacked out.

I was gone. I drifted through darkness, eventually coming upon a faint light in the distance. The light moved swiftly toward me, and when it reached me, it transformed into the figure of a woman who looked familiar, though I couldn't place her. She reached a hand out to touch mine, caressing it in such a loving, comforting way that it reminded me of being in the arms of my own mother, in the innocence of youth. I felt safe and loved, fully believing, for the first time in a long time, that I would be okay.

Then she said to me the words that changed my life forever: "No ... Not yet. There's more work to do." Then she let go of my hand and disappeared as quickly as she'd come.

Like a patient receiving an electrical jolt from a defibrillator, I startled awake and took an enormous gasp of air. I realized that my plan had failed. I was trapped, once again, in this miserable life. My strength completely drained and my mind emptied, I could do nothing but cry.

I was ready for it to stop. I was ready to take a stand for me. To either move forward together or move forward alone. I was glad that Josh was willing to come with me, to take on life again. There comes a time when we each get to Take A Stand for something we either get to say or do that will have a positive effect on you, those around you and possibly the world. It could be a very difficult thing to do because the answer may or may not be how you want it to look. Trust your intuition and follow your heart and you can get through it.

After hours passed this way, I heard the familiar sound of Lisa's keys in the door. It was time to face her and the desolation I'd created. I lay on the couch in the living room, holding my breath and waiting for the inevitable dressing down I knew I deserved.

She slowly made her way through the house, and spied the rifle in the hallway. I heard a slight gasp before she appeared, standing above me, looking down.

The look in her eyes was a mixture of pity and strength. She stood there in full uniform, badge over her heart and gun strapped to her side, and she looked different to me now. There was resolve in her eyes, watering with the enormity of what she was seeing, but I could see by the expression of distaste and disregard on her face that she was done with all this. Lisa, the strong, determined Lisa I'd fallen in love with, was once again standing here before me. I felt relieved to see her, even as I dreaded what would surely come next.

She sighed heavily, then looked me right in the eyes and said, "Josh, either you go to treatment *now*, or I'm packing my bags and leaving you."

I had been searching for a lifeline for a long time. I had wanted it all to stop, but didn't know how. Lisa's strength to call an end to all of this created the change we both wanted. That night, I left for rehab.

Fighting My Way Back

I was no stranger to the rehabilitation process. In my unusual youth, I was forced into youth behavioral and drug treatment programs twice. Even on my own, I had attempted a few times to quit partying, rarely with any long-lasting success. But before long, the cycle of nightclub work became too strong a force to confront sober. Once, as a preteen, and again at 13, I had even spent time in rehab, but I can see now I hadn't fully committed to the process; my family's business, my insecurity, and the resulting depression seemed to be good enough excuses to get off the wagon.

But there was something I had in late 2001 that I hadn't had those times before: I had a marriage I very much wanted to save. As much as I thought I loved drinking, I loved Lisa more. Our future was at stake, and I knew that if I were to lose Lisa, I would go over the edge and likely never come back. So it was with a new sense of strength, purpose, commitment, and a vision for the future that Lisa drove me to the Southern California rehabilitation center where I checked myself in at the end of November 2001.

Today, as I tell this story, I am amazed by the events that prompted me to escape the death I was surely facing. Many of my friends from that time in my life did not fare so well, and are now either dead, incarcerated, or still entangled in the web of addiction. I was fortunate to have found an incredibly supportive, loving wife, checked into the best possible rehab for my situation, and encountered the right teachers. The deck was stacked against me, and yet I got another chance, one I didn't believe I deserved.

I am now a successful, prosperous business owner, mentor, husband, father, friend, and contributor to life. But even after all this time, I know that checking into rehab that day was the best investment I have ever made.

That 28 days taught me how to turn my problems – problems I had believed were insurmountable – into solutions that put me on a path of healing, forgiveness, and happiness. I began to get at the root of my addiction, tracing issues like my own feelings of inadequacy and fear of failure back to my childhood. I took an inventory of my life and my fears, grappling with each one of them in order to divest it of its power. In a difficult month's time, I emerged a changed man, whole-heartedly committed to starting my life anew, clean and sober, and to continuing to shed the baggage that had landed me here in the first place. And I knew the process had only just begun.

Over the course of that month, I also developed a number of friendships. In a community so close-knit and reliant upon each other, so connected by troubles as we were, you couldn't help but form friendships. One of mine was with the owner of the treatment center, Chris Spencer (whom I just called Spencer), a recovering alcoholic himself who had turned his life around and dedicated himself to serving other addicts.

Early on in my stay, as he and I got to talking, I shared with him a little about my story – about my "family business," and what it was like running nightclubs in Vegas. Spencer said we had something in common; he, too, had worked for a number of years in the service industry. He had, in fact, owned a chain of restaurants. We compared experiences, discussing the fact that the service industry is a breeding ground for people like us.

"Back when I was drinking, all I wanted to do was open up restaurants," Spencer said, rubbing his chin and chuckling as he recalled those days. Then he looked right at me. "Now that I'm sober, all I want to do is open up treatment centers." Then he stood up, patted me on the back, and said, "Maybe you'll want to do the same thing." I chuckled too, and shook my head, dismissing the notion.

Lisa and I did a lot of healing work together through the program, and she had driven down for a weekend to attend sessions with me and my counselor. And we had been able to talk a lot on the phone about what I was going through.

When she arrived to pick me up on my last day, I felt a mixture of relief and joy over seeing her, sadness about leaving what had been a safe haven for the last month, and growing dread over returning to Las Vegas, the site of my destruction.

Before setting out on the five-hour drive home, we stopped at the Dana Point home of my stepbrother (and namesake of my workplace), Dylan, where a holiday party was in progress. While it was nice to be surrounded by family, it didn't take long for an uncomfortable silence to settle over the party after our arrival. It seemed no one quite knew what to say. I was eager to share my rehab experience with the group, and reveal all the things I'd learned, but when I'd broach the subject, my family members seemed either to visibly squirm with discomfort or act

I was proud of Josh for taking this on and he is correct that we did a lot of healing work. I was surprised how easy it was for me to forgive and let go. I was so ready to move forward and have this heavy burden of addiction, this heavy weight of anger, sadness, and pain go away that when we processed with his therapist, I was able to let it go quickly. I hadn't felt that good in years and I knew that letting go and not holding resentments on the past would enable us to have a brighter future. If just he healed and I did nothing, our relationship would still be unhealthy. Learning from, forgiving and healing the past is an important part of personal development and being able to move forward successfully in your future. Sometimes we don't know what we have to let go of. If you are stuck, take a good look at your past to see what has to be cleared.

altogether dismissive, as if to say, "Sure, Josh, that sounds great. But we'll see." Of course, they'd seen me go down this road a few times, so it was understandable that they would be cautious. After all, we had all made a living from selling alcohol and partying. It was awkward to challenge the very thing that was putting roofs over our heads and food on our tables.

Still I was anxious to get going. After dinner and opening our gifts, Lisa and I packed up and readied ourselves to make a quick exit. We said our goodbyes, exchanged a few hugs, and headed out into the night.

"Wait! Josh! Hold up!" called my dad, who was running down the front steps with a box in his hand. "I forgot this! I wanted to give you both something." He reached us and stretched his arm out to hand me the brown cardboard shipping box. I looked quizzically at my dad, then ripped off the tab to open the box, revealing a purple and gold box entitled *You Can Choose to Be Rich*. A slick, salesy photo of the author, Robert T. Kiyosaki, smiled at me from the cover of this set of audiobook CDs.

With a half-hearted smile, I said, "Thanks, Dad," and handed the box to Lisa with a subtle eye roll. My dad had a habit of buying his kids things he'd seen on infomercials – useless and overly complex exercise gear, motivational programs, gadgets that didn't work. He'd get caught up in the excitement of the ad and want to share it with us, but it always seemed to miss the mark. This gift, I thought, would be no different.

My dad read all that in my expression. As if reading my mind, he said, "This guy is different, Josh. You'll like him. I promise." Then, after waiting a beat to see if I would come around, he added, "He's from Hawaii," as if that tiny connection would seal my interest.

"Okay, Dad, thanks," I said.

Then, in his deepest, most authoritative voice – the boss voice – he said, "Son, promise me you'll listen to these, okay?"

I gave him my word that I would, tossed the CD set into the back seat of the car, and we were on our way.

I initially resented the gift and had no intention of listening to it. I fidgeted in my seat for a few minutes, sighing, until Lisa finally broke the stalemate. "Oh, let's just listen to them already. I know it's going to bug you until you do."

So for the entire drive home to Las Vegas, rather than worrying about what lay ahead for me here after my month of clearing my head and beginning to rebuild our marriage, our heads filled instead with thoughts of hope and inspiration, ideas about having better, more fulfilling, more prosperous lives that were in no way connected to drinking, bars, violence, or nightclubs.

Thus began our journey, literally and figuratively. On the drive back to Las Vegas, as we listened to Robert and Kim Kiyosaki share their philosophies about money, life, and learning, we realized that this program was nothing like we'd expected. We assumed that the CDs were just about how we could get rich by buying something from them, or repeating some mantra garbage we'd heard dozens of times before. But, as we began to understand, the *Rich Dad* message was completely different. It was a life shift, or, as Robert says, a "context shift."

Normally, when we traveled, we listened to audiobooks by people like Steven King and Tom Clancy. It was a great way to keep us entertained and make the time pass quickly. But the idea of learning and improving our lives while traveling had never crossed our minds. Continuing education was, in our minds, a concept reserved for people in school, studying for exams. But here we were, in our car, learning far more than either of us had ever learned in a classroom. Entertaining and distracting our minds was a goal we no longer aspired to – we'd had enough of that.

We pulled into our driveway before the program had finished, but instead of turning it off and getting out of the car, we sat there for nearly 25 minutes in the darkened car until it had finished. And afterward, we remained silent, much like that afternoon in 1999, after seeing *The Matrix*. After watching the movie on that day two years prior, we had both been thinking the same thing – that our lifestyle was unsustainable and unfulfilling. That much we knew. But we hadn't had the motivation or understanding to make a change.

Life is a journey of learning; look at the books, shows and activities that you do. Are they supporting you in continuous growth or hindering you? Is there something you can add or change to your daily routine to keep learning? All the successful people I know are always learning something new that adds value to their life and those around them.

Now here we were in late 2001, and once again we were both thinking the same thing. Only this time, instead of the painful realization that we were stuck in a matrix of our own making, our realization was one of hope. We actually did have a choice, one that Robert Kiyosaki had just revealed to us.

Our choice was this: We could keep doing what we'd been doing, or we could take a leap of faith. We could embark on a new path, one of personal development and transformation. We had already begun that path while I was in rehab, and had no interest in going back to where we'd started. Returning to our old lives seemed impossible from this new vantage point.

We were squarely at an intersection of two paths that day, and we chose to be rich, like Robert Kiyosaki, and not just in a way that implied money. We wanted to live rich, *thoroughly* rich, in health, wealth, *and* happiness. We wanted to do work that mattered, that filled us with satisfaction and joy, one that would bring us together and enable us to continue learning every single day so that we would always feel like we did at that moment in our driveway.

By the time we stepped into our house that night, I had resolved that I couldn't, and wouldn't, work in my father's nightclub business anymore.

We would create a new life for ourselves, one that would mean assisting others to get through and overcome the painful experience of addiction. That was the very beginning of Journey Healing Centers. At that moment, we committed to becoming Social Capitalists.

Chapter Thought

If you were to take a leap of faith, to follow your heart, your passion, and your intuition, what could happen? What would the results of this be five years from now? And if you did nothing, what would those results be in five years?

Chapter Two

Understanding
Social Capitalism

"Indeed, for anyone who has ever said, 'This isn't working' or 'We can do better!'—for anyone who gets a kick out of challenging the status quo, shaking up the system, or practicing a little entrepreneurial 'creative destruction'—these are propitious times."

—David Bornstein, *How to Change the World*

Perhaps to best define the concept of Social Capitalism, we should turn to one of its pioneers.

J. Gregory Dees, adjunct professor and founding faculty director of the Center for the Advancement of Social Entrepreneurship (CASE) at Duke University's Fuqua School of Business, is considered an academic leader in the area of social entrepreneurship. In 2006, at a gathering hosted by New Profit Inc., Dees said that the term "social entrepreneur" conveys "this blending of sectors—a mixture of the social purpose we typically associate with nonprofits and the kind of entrepreneurial orientation we associate with business, particularly with the most creative and dynamic aspect of business."

In other words, social entrepreneurs build businesses that make sense while accomplishing social missions.

Of course, the concept of becoming social entrepreneurs wasn't anywhere on our radar in late 2001. Once we'd made our decision to creating a new life for ourselves, that was just the beginning of the journey. As any entrepreneur in any industry can tell you, bridging the gap between the glimmer of an idea and getting a successful, full-fledged business up and running is where most new businesses fall short, social or not.

Once we'd realized that we wanted to create this new life for ourselves *and* be financially free, we had to come to grips with the idea that we had a long, hard road ahead of us. We didn't have to change a few things in our lives... We had to change *everything*, from the self-defeating thoughts we had to the words we used, the friends we spent time with and the things we did in our free time. For that moment in our driveway, we felt as if we'd figured things out, which was a relief. We were ready to embrace change, no matter how difficult the road that lay ahead.

But then the full weight of what that decision implied fell upon us.

As much as we would like to say that we were so moved by my experience in rehab and the idea of taking control over our lives that we instantly knew our lifelong passion, it wouldn't be the truth. We didn't decide to open rehabilitation centers as we were driving back to Las Vegas from Southern California. What we were most passionate about was rebuilding our lives and our marriage.

We were just two people heading back from a rehab center to a clean start, determined not to let the clubs and money and destructive lifestyle we'd fallen into reclaim us. But I was still my father's right-hand man, employed at a nightclub, and as much as I didn't want to live that life anymore, I had no idea what life I *did* want. And sharing this with my father, a man who would likely take such an admission as an act of weakness, was simply not an option that I saw as viable. I was terrified to return to work, but terrified not to.

I'd been home for only a couple of days when I found myself standing on the floor of Dylan's, surrounded by the more than 1,500 people celebrating New Year's Eve, 2001. All night I had been wondering what the hell I was doing there. I felt beaten and trapped. I watched the smiles and laughter of the people partying around me, and as the night wore on, it became clear to me that it was all fake, a big lie. I don't know, perhaps I was projecting my issues onto them, but at that moment, it occurred to me that very few of those people were honestly happy. As I watched the ball begin to drop in Times Square on the big-screen TVs on every wall, and heard the seconds counting down to the beginning of a brand-new year, I felt my fear of separating from my father's business eroding in the face of the fear I felt about spending another year in that place. Nothing, *nothing*, not the threat of my often-violent and temperamental father, not the threat of financial ruin, not the uncertainty about my future career or the potential estrangement from my family, none of it was worth living like this, in the midst of that toxic environment. *I had to GET OUT.* Immediately.

Meanwhile, Lisa was facing her own fears as the clock ticked down to midnight and she walked the Vegas Strip in uniform with her fellow officers that New Year's Eve. The crowds, hundreds of thousands strong, could have easily been dangerous enough, but Lisa's fears had more to do with what was happening to me, a very newly recovering alcoholic, in a nightclub, on this night in which it seemed the entire world was focused on drinking and partying. She knew I had to get out of the nightclub business, because all it would have taken was doing one celebratory shot with a customer to drag me back. She carried a knot of worry around in her stomach all night.

After the night wound down and the sun began to rise, our shifts came to an end and it was time to finally clock out. When we were both home safe and sound from our jobs, she was surprised, relieved, excited, and nervous to learn of my decision on the morning of New Year's Day to begin my extracting myself from my father's business. We made the decision that morning to start fresh. This was it. We didn't know what we were going to do, but we *did* know that if we didn't act right then and there, we might never get out. We spent New Year's Day joyfully brainstorming the possibilities

> *Your environment can be supportive or destructive to who you are and what you want to do. If you want to change, you get to look at your environment and make it one that supports you.*

that might await us. It felt somehow taboo for me to consider doing anything else besides working in my dad's nightclub business, or for Lisa not to be a commissioned officer, but yet it also felt so right, so thrilling to realize that a whole world of possibilities was out there for the taking. Lisa and I just threw everything that popped into our heads onto the table for discussion that day, no holds barred.

Then, in a flash, my discussion with Spencer popped into my mind – Spencer, the former restaurateur who decided to open rehab centers when he realized that the restaurant business no longer suited his sobriety.

Could that have been a sign? Did we dare to dream a similar life for ourselves? Yes, we did. Because as soon as I shared the memory of that conversation out loud with Lisa, we both grew silent and looked at each other, completely serious. We recognized what felt like a calling. After all, we knew what it was like for other people grappling with addiction, and we also knew what their loved ones were going through. The puzzle pieces of our lives all seemed to come together right at that moment, and we could see how everything that had happened to us might have happened for a reason.

Because *of course* it made sense. I had done rehab several times, I knew what worked and what didn't. Lisa and I had both known the pain of addiction, the difficulty in returning to life sober, the systems that must be in place to stay clean and sober. It would be incredibly rewarding to share what we knew in order to keep others on the straight and narrow, to give families back the peace that Lisa and I were just coming to know and love.

We made the decision to sleep on it, and to call Spencer the next morning. I did, first thing. I shared with what we had been experiencing—my feeling of being trapped at the nightclubs and my certainty that, spiritually, it would be suicide for me to continue to work there. I told him how it was just a matter of time before I succumbed to that environment again. I shared how Lisa felt the same way, and was in full support of my decision to leave.

I told Spencer that we wanted to be part of the solution, and could no longer be part of the problem. Then, I asked Spencer if he could teach me about the rehab business, and told him I would appreciate his support and guidance.

"Are you serious about this?" he asked me.

I assured him that, yes, I was absolutely serious.

"Well, okay, great!" he said. "Be in my office Monday morning."

Without any idea where Spencer was leading us or whether there was a hidden agenda, I drove back to Southern California to meet with him and gather every little bit of insight and advice I possibly could from this man who had walked the same path that Lisa and I wanted to embark on.

Our meeting lasted all of ten minutes, during which time he handed me a stack of policy and procedure manuals for his rehab centers, and said, "Here. This is how you open a treatment center." In fact, he shared proprietary information with me, to the dismay of his staff.

"Getting licensed is one of the hardest things to do in this business," he said, handing me some more paperwork. "Here's how you do it."

I stood there, gracious but in shock, holding the growing stack of 3-ring binders Spencer's kept piling on me. When he'd handed over everything, he said, in a tone that sounded as if he were giving an order to an employee, "I want you to fly to Florida to see my treatment center there. Okay? I'll be there in a few days, so I'll see you there and we can talk some more." And without so much as a handshake to wish me well, he was out the door to his next appointment.

"How'd it go?" Lisa asked me when I returned home later that night.

"Well, it was a great ten minutes," I told her, stunned by how good I still felt in our plan, and buoyed by the tools Spencer had provided to me and his seeming confidence in my ability to pull it off. He hadn't seemed to question me or our decision at all. "Lisa, maybe it's because we asked for his support rather than just taking from him. I don't know. But now, we get to go to Florida."

Fortunately, she trusted me and this new mentor of mine, Spencer, enough that she was willing to hop on board a plane to Florida along with me. There was absolutely no hesitation from either of us. We booked our flights for a week in Florida with our own money, and completely, willingly submitted to Spencer's directives. Later we discovered that he and his associates had only scheduled about one full day's worth of meetings for us, involving travel to several locations around Orlando and talks with many people who were experienced in the addiction treatment industry.

Looking back, we're convinced that this was Spencer's test to determine how serious we actually were about this decision. And it appeared that we'd passed.

By the end of the day, we were only more convinced of our decision, and were eager to hit the ground running. However, we had booked a week in Florida. So after the day with Spencer was complete, we decided to take a few days out for ourselves before this new venture and visit Disneyworld. It was during this time that our daughter, Haley, was conceived. We took it as a universal sign, the third in a series of signs that included my near-death experience and my dad's providential Christmas gift, that told us we were about to begin the life we were meant for.

We had years of management and leadership experience between the two of us, a solid foundation of financial education through *Rich Dad,* the policy and procedure manuals containing information about licensing, a supportive colleague and mentor, and, I was shocked to realize, my father's blessing to separate from his business and begin our own. Everything seemed to be pointing us in this direction.

The Foundation for Success

Over the next couple of years, we were involved in the long process of establishing Journey Healing Centers. We set about on a challenging journey that included securing capital, finding a location for our business, becoming licensed as a treatment facility, establishing a niche market, finding and growing a clientele, enhancing our variety of services, and expanding our territory by adding locations. How that all happened is a story we'll be sharing with you.

We were successful, eventually, but we had to make a lot of mistakes along the way. We faced a lot of challenges and had to continually remind ourselves of what we wanted and why. We had to recommit dozens of times – times when it would have been a lot easier to throw up our hands and say, "Forget it, let's do something else."

But when it came right down to it, what we cared most about was being part of the solution by serving the roughly 140 million people around the world who struggle with dependence on alcohol. In 2002, when we were in the beginning stages of creating our business, we found that more than 80 percent of people who needed addictions treatment didn't receive it.

Many people give up before they reach their goals, learn to find your strength and determination to keep going. Evaluate how serious you are about your passion and dreams and make sure it is what you truly want.

We found that addiction affects every culture and every socioeconomic class; it does not discriminate. This mission was deeply personal for us, and we had a strong "why" for building this socially conscious business.

From that passion and deep sense of personal commitment grew a series of steps that we believe to be the foundation of a social enterprise:

- **Discover your "why" – build upon your passion.** Our "why" wasn't instantly clear to us. But after going through the clarifying process of rehab (others may find the experience of personal development seminars similarly helpful), it became very clear. Then, our "why" was all we had, and it was the reason we got up every morning and kept working on this business. That's still true today. Your "why" is everything. Having a strong "why" will keep going when times get tough, as they will from time to time in your business.

- **Make and clarify your commitment.** We'd made the commitment to open a treatment center. We clarified our commitment by uncovering research, both from Spencer and data we collected on our own about the legalities of doing this kind of work, what it took to be licensed, the facts about treatment and recovery, and what did and didn't work in terms of running a successful facility. We invested every free hour of our time in research, and turned our home office into a "mission control" center where we collected all the pieces of information we uncovered and filed away for later use. And we assessed our own strengths and weaknesses, taking into account how our own personal experiences could show us what values weren't currently being met in the world of addiction treatment.

- **Find the right support system, mentors, and coaches.** We already had Spencer in our corner, mentoring us and offering us wisdom when he could. We would encounter many more mentors and supporters in the coming years, and they would prove to be invaluable for us. The right support system, mentor, and coach will push you to be uncomfortable. He or she will push you beyond what you thought was possible, get you to think differently. This is a sign of a great support system. If they aren't supporting your vision and pushing you along the way, you deserve someone else, because otherwise you may never achieve what you want out of life.

- **Dedicate and invest in yourself.** We invested a tremendous amount of time, money, and energy into personal development. Your business and your life will be a reflection of you. Mahatma Gandhi once said, "For things to change, first I must change." A business will only grow to the capacity of the owner's context. You can suppress the growth of your business or you can lead it to success. We have never stopped dedicating time to improving ourselves and the work we do. This wasn't something we did in our free time; it is part of the business plan.

- **Get a financial education.** When we were first starting out, the two of us knew very little about what money really is, how to raise capital, how to make investments, or the difference between active and passive income. The key to beginning our financial education was *Choose To Be Rich*, but that was only the beginning. Bottom line, it became clear very early on that regardless of your social mission, you can't run a successful business without respecting the power of financial education. Continue to learn as the business grows; as the world and economies change, there is always more to know.

- **Build a business plan.** Here's where you really get to think through the business design. Is the business leverageable, financeable, expandable, and predictable? No one will give you capital to build your business if you cannot show (on paper, at least) that you have invested time, energy, and resources into thinking through your business, its mission, the team members involved, and how you are going to return investors' capital. This is where the rubber meets the road in terms of a social enterprise's viability.

As it turns out, the steps we took to lay a solid foundation in our business align pretty neatly with those recommended by many of the major players in the social entrepreneurship sector.

In fact, in a November 2002 report by CASE entitled *The Process of Social Entrepreneurship: Creating Opportunities Worthy of Serious Pursuit,* Authors Ayse Guclu, J. Gregory Dees, and Beth Battle Anderson say that personal experience usually drives the formation of social enterprises. That is followed by a determination of social need, or "the gaps between socially desirable conditions and the existing reality." Then, because a social needs assessment often over-emphasizes the negative, social entrepreneurs determine where the assets are that can be "leveraged to create wealth." Finally, they create change, and are constantly inspired by it, seeking opportunities to have a positive social impact.

"Successful social entrepreneurs embody this 'how can' attitude, particularly in the idea generation phase," say Guclu, Dees, and Anderson. "Effective social entrepreneurs carry this orientation into the opportunity development process, engaging in continuous innovation, adaptation, analysis, and learning along the way."

Really, this is, and was, a major key to our success—this process of "engaging in continuous innovation, adaptation, and learning along the way."

Mirjam Schöning, the head of the Schwab Foundation for Social Entrepreneurship, a global organization whose mission is to highlight and advance leading models of sustainable social innovation, has identified seven basic tenets or pieces of advice for social entrepreneurs, after having worked in the sector for ten years:

1. Follow your passion – it's the most important ingredient, and it's what will keep you going in the tough times.

2. Balance your passion with rationale. Are you addressing a real, substantiated need?

3. Brainstorm – generate a thousand ideas, and don't be afraid to consider them, refine them, dismiss them, or replace them.

4. Carefully choose your business model, and articulate your vision, mission, and systems for evaluation and measurement from day one.

5. Study approaches that lead to the same impact you're trying to achieve. Is your idea really as unique as you think? Consider the competitive landscape.

6. Consider franchising your social enterprise – it's arguable that what we need most is for entrepreneurs to take their brilliant ideas to other parts of the world.

7. Give yourself a minimum of three years (or 36 months, which sounds shorter) to get your enterprise off the ground and into calmer waters.

Perhaps, for us, the fact that the life we were leaving behind would have killed me eventually is what kept us at it night and day, working on this business despite the obstacles. We literally felt as if we had no choice. Like a frog in tepid water that is slowly cooked as the pot works its way to a boil, I could see myself dying a little every single day I remained a nightclub employee. And despite Lisa's respectable profession and the contribution she made each day, as an officer, to the social good, it often left her unsatisfied and craving a more significant outlet in which she could improve our lives and the lives of those around us.

So, perhaps, that's the real key to a successful social enterprise: The fact that doing *nothing* about a problem or injustice, or failing to address it properly, affects a lot more people than just you.

For-Profit or Nonprofit?

You certainly don't have to create a business to begin solving problems. Plenty of people join the Peace Corps or Doctors Without Borders. It's wonderful to donate money to, or volunteer for, the Sierra Club, The Nature Conservancy, Feed the Children, Feeding America, The Green Children Foundation, or any other charitable organization, and lots of amazing people do this. It's much needed, and we would hate to disparage those important efforts by indicating somehow that this kind of selfless act should be supplanted by a for-profit business model with profit being the ultimate goal.

Journey Healing Centers stemmed from our desire to create an environment that supported life and made us a living while we were doing something important to assist others. But that's not to say that the efforts of volunteers and nonprofit organizations are somehow less worthy.

We will say, however, that the desire to give back to the world or to solve a social problem need not be relegated to the nonprofit or non-governmental organization (NGO) realm. What many people, like us, are discovering is that not only are the desires for being of service and earning a profit no longer mutually exclusive, but that in many cases, the for-profit model is more sustainable and powerful over the long term. After all, anyone who controls your funding ultimately controls you. By having a for-profit, we can expand the business to be more responsive, provide a much-needed service to humanity in all socioeconomic class, and give more easily to other charities through doing our work in a free market with fewer regulatory constrictions.

One believer of this premise is Michael Holthouse, a Texas-based philanthropist and longtime entrepreneur who was founder and president of Paranet, Inc., a computer network services company established in 1990. He was an *Inc. Magazine* Entrepreneur of the Year and two-time "Inc. 500 Fastest Growing Company" winner. After selling Paranet to Sprint in 1997, Holthouse channeled his energies and financial resources into philanthropic projects, including the Holthouse Foundation For Kids, a foundation that focuses on proactive and experiential programs for at-risk youth, and Prepared 4 Life, a nonprofit that operates Lemonade Day, an experiential, community-based program that develops life skills; and teaches youth about the skills and values of entrepreneurship through the formation of lemonade stands.

"There are lots of 501(c)3's out there that are currently operating off the kind of model that says, 'I'm doing good in the world, but I've got to go to foundations and get money from them in order to keep doing what I'm doing,'" says Holthouse. "But that model is a dinosaur, and it isn't going to last much longer. Every group that wants to address a social issue is going to have to operate like a real business. They'll have to operate with budgets, revenues, and services that they provide. They'll have to operate as any business would. The profits may not be distributed to shareholders, but would be reinvested back into the organization so that it can increase the number of people it serves or improve the quality by which it serves people."

"I think social entrepreneurs share the trait that we don't think we should need to starve to make a difference," says R. Christine Hershey, president and founder of Hershey Cause, a strategic communications firm that works with social entrepreneurs and corporations to build brands and create campaigns that help advance social change. "One of the reasons we haven't solved the world's biggest problems is that folks in those sectors are underfunded."

It's why Hershey suggests that any social venture still be grounded in business best practices. "It's almost as if, in the old days, in the nonprofit model, there was a virtue that nonprofits didn't need to be vigorous, or think strategically. I think that's turned into a crutch. And I think that's why a lot of them are barely limping along. I think they need rigorous best practices to figure out how they'll survive and make a bigger contribution."

The Obama Administration has set forth world food security as a top priority in its foreign policy plans, but rather than relying on NGOs to handle this, the administration has shared that a for-profit philosophy can be the change-maker. A February 2011 article in Voice of America News (VOANews.com) relates a story about Mozambique's poultry farming practices. Because farmers there couldn't afford medicines or enough food to properly raise chickens, the chickens they produced were often spoiled or too thin to compete on a global scale with other foreign producers.

When TechnoServe, a non-governmental organization based in Washington, D.C. that provides business development assistance to aid in breaking the cycle of poverty in third-world countries, and Cargill, an agribusiness corporation, got involved with financial, regulatory, and business development support, the quality of poultry raised in Mozambique drastically improved. It created jobs, improved incomes for farmers, and ultimately improved the quality of poultry that Cargill could then sell, which in turn bolstered its bottom line. The motive for profit became a win-win-win – for farmers, for industry, and for consumers – while ultimately accomplishing a major step in the fight for world food security.

What we found as we started Journey Healing Centers is that we really prefer to have control over ourselves and how we run the business. We decided to run it as a true, revenue-generating business so that we could continue to reinvest in the very best services and treatments for our customers. How could we expect to attract the very best addiction counselors and doctors by relying on the nonprofit model of relying on kind donations of time from busy professionals?

The triple-bottom-line philosophy comes up frequently in discussions of social entrepreneurship. The three prongs of this triple bottom line are typically referred to as "the 3 P's": People, Planet, and Profit. Social enterprises aspire to a bottom line that achieves social mission, benefits or does no harm to the planet, and still earns a profit.

For us, our triple bottom line morphed into **"social value, profit, and freedom"**—that is, providing social value, profit that enables us to continue doing it, and freedom from the shackles of addiction and a destructive lifestyle, not only for ourselves but for those we treat as well. And, as we learned more about moving from employees to business owners and, ultimately, investors, we earned financial freedom as well.

It's important to note, though, that the term "Social Capitalist" might imply that we were somehow all about money—that because we embraced the *Rich Dad* philosophies of growing wealth, we were somehow looking to capitalize on others' misery in order to grow wealthy.

The truth is that if money were our motive, I would have stayed in the nightclub business. It certainly could provide a lavish lifestyle. I could eventually have taken over for my father and run and expanded a very successful nightclub operation. Lisa and I volunteer for Journey Healing Centers; we have never taken a paycheck from the company.

From Day 1, we have invested money back into the business to improve, expand, and enhance its offerings. And we have established a toll-free, 24-hour addiction hotline, run by a call center that operates 7 days a week and takes calls from anyone looking for support, advice, or resources, regardless of whether the callers are seeking treatment from JHC.

And the truth is that it's okay to be profitable while helping the world. In fact, as global trends seem to indicate, it may be preferable.

Chapter Thought

How would you characterize your relationship with money? Do you curse it because you don't have enough? Do you speak poorly of those people who have it? Money is only an idea. If you change your thoughts about money, you can change how you relate to it. Money was designed to serve you, not for you to serve it.

Chapter Three

The Growing Social Entrepreneur Movement

"I think the new focus on social entrepreneurship is an expression of pragmatism as much as idealism. It is being driven, in part, by disappointed idealists who became disenchanted with the ability of large-scale government programs to solve social problems."

—J. Gregory Dees, *The Past, Present, and Future of Social Entrepreneurship*

In the spring of 2001 in South Bend, Indiana, Christopher Fuchs (or "Kreece," as his friends know him) and F. Xavier Helgesen were taking stock of what they were going to do now that they'd graduated from the University of Notre Dame with their respective degrees in mechanical engineering and information systems. The dot-com bubble had just burst, and things looked pretty bleak in the start-up world.

Meanwhile, Kreece looked around the apartment he and Xavier shared with another graduate, and became frustrated by the volume of old, by-now useless textbooks that the three had accumulated, and which now sat in piles in its various corners. They certainly were valuable—he'd paid enough for them in the first place—and he could probably sell them back to the campus bookstore. But the chance of getting back what the books were actually worth was slim, and Kreece knew the possibilities that the up-and-coming Internet marketplace offered.

"Xavier told me about Half.com, and sure enough, I sold my books for about $20 or $30 each—books that would otherwise have been just trashed, or in some cases burned, which is what many student I knew had done when they'd gotten frustrated," Kreece remembers.

Kreece ended up making about $400 on his own textbooks, and Xavier had similar success with his own books and those of their roommate. What if they could collect books en masse from around campus and sell them, too—could that become a business?

"We talked to a friend who worked at the Robinson Community Learning Center, and found out they were looking to raise funds for an after-school reading program," says Kreece. "We came up with the idea that if students would part with them and drop them off and work with us, we could ensure that something good was being done with them."

They ran the idea past Jay, the center's director, who went for the proposal: Kreece and Xavier would handle collecting the books, storing them, and selling them, and then they would split the proceeds in half with the center. So in winter of 2001, Kreece and Xavier began a book drive, using boxes they'd collected from the local recycling center and posters strategically placed around campus, and within six months they'd collected about 2,500 books.

"We spent the better part of summer on it," Kreece says. "I was tutoring that summer and auditing some classes, and I was planning on going back to med school. Xavier was doing some international traveling. So it was a side project to list and sell books, and it took us a long time to inventory them—basically the whole summer on a part-time basis. I'll never forget it ... It took me about four or five tries to get the columns right and everything on Amazon, and, long story short, finally I was able to get about 2,100-odd books listed. And a few minutes later, I got an email with an order. I went to the shelf where our inventory system said it was, pulled the book, and I ran over to my house to tell my new roommates I had sold a book. When I got back, I had sold five or ten more. That week was a blur of shipping books."

At the end of the summer, Kreece and Xavier had sold more than $20,000 worth of books in one month's time, and were able to present the Robinson Center with a check for $10,000.

Now it looked like this could actually be a business. Encouraged by their success, and energized by the potential impact this could have, not only on their own finances or the Robinson Center, but for the cause of literacy, Kreece and Xavier drafted a business plan, with help from a friend and classmate, Jeff Kurtzman, who worked in investment banking. In April 2003, the three founders submitted the plan to a business plan competition at Notre Dame, and took first prize for "Best Social Venture," an award that earned them $7,000 in seed money to make their new venture, Book Drives for Better Lives, a reality on campuses throughout the country.

Kreece took his MCAT the day after the final presentation at the business plan competition, assuming that he'd eventually proceed with his plan to attend medical school. But the potential this venture offered needed to be explored. "That check got us a lot of recognition, and a lot of confidence," Kreece recalls. "We boot-strapped the company for the first few years, so $7,000 went a long way for us."

That competition did something else for those young men: It introduced them to judge David Murphy, who became a trusted guide and mentor, offering advice about business development that became so useful, they asked him to come on board as CEO, which he did in 2004.

Kreece, Xavier, and Jeff brought on a few people to help out with the venture, which began growing rapidly on college campuses. And they added new partner recipients to their list, supporting global literacy by providing books to Books for Africa, to keep schools in those countries stocked with textbooks.

Then, Xavier discovered that libraries around the country were wrestling with a perpetual problem. Apparently, when new, popular books become available and are added to their inventories, libraries are often forced to make room on the shelves by discarding old library books. "Some of them told us stories about running to dumpsters in the middle of the night with books because they didn't have space," says Kreece.

They realized that by partnering with libraries to collect their old, discarded books, they could contribute useful books and proceeds from their sales to literacy groups around the world. Now they had their triple-bottom line: They were helping the cause of literacy (People), keeping valuable books out of landfills (Planet), and raising money, too, in a business model that provided equity sharing and competitive benefits (Profit).

Additionally, BWB was the industry's first business to use a Carbon Neutral Shopping Cart, with a few cents being collected during each checkout to pay for renewable energy credits and reforestation projects.

"I thought I'd put med school off for a couple of years, but obviously that's become indefinite," says Kreece, reflecting on the triple-bottom-line social enterprise which, in September 2003, became incorporated as Better World Books, Inc. "I felt more drawn to this, so I shelved med school."

Though the company has grown rapidly and is now a 130-person operation with more than two million new and used books for sale, it still retains its original mission: collecting books people don't want, selling them, and using that money to improve literacy worldwide. The bulk of their books still come from more than 1,200 college campuses across the U.S., though now Better World Books also partners with roughly 1,000 local libraries to sell their old books and then give back a percentage of the proceeds. Little green donation bins placed in communities around the country collect any and all books people are willing to part with, and whatever can't be sold is recycled. Roughly 400,000-500,000 books are collected each week, and through BWB's large-scale operation located in Mishawaka, Indiana, roughly 5 million books each year are sent to schools across Africa through Books for Africa and Feed the Children.

"We've made a commitment to donate a book for every book sold through our website," explains Kreece. "When we sell books, it keeps us sustainable; we pay for shipping, processing, everything in between in order to run the operation."

Kreece says that in November 2011, BWB reached an important milestone: Since the company's inception, it had raised $10 million for literacy and library organizations. "We're looking for additional outlets, and we have plenty of good books to get into the hands of those who can't afford them or don't have access."

The BWB business model has earned more than a dozen awards and accolades, including the 2008 Fast Company/Monitor Group Social Capitalist Award; the 2009 *Business Week* Most Promising Social Entrepreneur of the Year; recognition from *Time Magazine* in 2009 as one of the Top 25 Responsibility Pioneers (in the United States); the 2009 Waste Wise Gold Award for Paper Reduction and the 2010 Waste Wise Gold Award in Climate Change, both from the Environmental Protection Agency; distinction as a Top eTailer by Internet Retailer in 2010; selection as #96 on the list of Business Insider's Digital 100: The World's Most Valuable Startups in 2010; ranking as one of the six "Rockstars of the New Economy" by B Lab in 2012; and selection as one of the twenty companies ranked "Best for the World" in the B Corp Annual Report by B Lab in 2012.

The Social Entrepreneurship Wave

Better World Books, Inc. is considered today to be one of the major players in the social entrepreneurship space, having caught the wave as it was only beginning to gather momentum in the middle of the first decade of the millennium. But as Kreece Fuchs is quick to point out, that was purely coincidence. "People have recognized us as being one of the leading social enterprises, and we didn't even know what we were getting into. We *did* know we could leverage books with life left in them and do some good from them."

We certainly didn't intend to enter the realm of Social Capitalism because it was a new, trendy thing to do, or because a lot of companies were jumping on that bandwagon. Neither did Chris Spencer, our mentor in the formation of our treatment center. "I had been a restaurant owner," he says, describing his impetus to form Spencer Recovery Centers. "Due to the mental illness of a person close to me, I decided to establish a service to help people who were mentally ill. I developed The River Community to help dual-diagnosis patients with treatment and housing." Spencer Recovery Centers was opened soon after, when Spencer realized the close ties between mental illness and addiction.

At some point, Spencer aims to become a non-profit entity, in order to provide affordable treatment options while continuing to increase alcohol and drug abuse awareness through the media. For right now, however, the for-profit model enables him to provide a valuable service.

"I think it's a lot easier to amass a lot of resources if you have something that can make a profit, and you can do so more quickly," says Xavier Helgesen, who has taken a more advisory role with BWB in the last year in order to fuel his entrepreneurial fire with other cause-based enterprises. "A nonprofit doesn't have the power to grow and fund-raise as fast. With a for-profit, you have the power to grow quickly, as long as your customers allow you to … NGOs and nonprofits play an important role, but a lot of it has to do with creativity. You have to be creative and decide how you're going to maximize profit. My preference has been to create profit-maximizing businesses that create good as a natural by-product. I think it's more about finding what you actually want to do and figuring out whether there's a way to make money doing it. If not, build a nonprofit, fund-raise, that's great, too. But I think the biggest social enterprise in the world might be Google, because social organizations improve the world by their existence and are absolutely profit-maximizing."

Though doing *good* and doing *well* have worked hand-in-hand throughout at least the last century, it only seems to have caught real fire over the last decade or so, likely because of companies like BWB, who, through the power of media and the Internet, have an incredible capacity to share their story with the masses.

However, some of the earliest social entrepreneurs included people like Susan B. Anthony, who spearheaded the fight for women's rights and the adoption of the 19th amendment; John Muir, a naturalist, conservationist, and writer who fought to protect Yosemite National Park, helped establish the National Park System, and helped found the Sierra Club; Dr. Maria Montessori, who developed the Montessori School approach to children's education; Florence Nightingale, who is considered the founder of modern nursing; Margaret Sanger, a family-planning leader who founded the Planned Parenthood Foundation of America; and Frederick

Law Olmstead, regarded as the father of the American profession of landscape architecture.

These days, some of the most noteworthy, innovative, and beloved business people and companies have a social consciousness: Tom's Shoes, with its "One for One" business model of providing a pair of shoes to a child in need for every new pair of shoes purchased; Patagonia, the outdoor apparel retailer that vigorously protects and polices the environment; Starbucks, with its responsibly grown, ethically traded coffee and strong support of farmers; Odwalla, with its

Being a part of the solution or being socially conscious can be a part of a business, the whole business, or even a hobby. Finding what you like and seeing how you can make it profitable and give back is what the world deserves right now. With so many people losing faith in governments it's up to the individuals to find their passion and make a difference.

environmentally friendly, locally sourced juices and bars that enable the company to make charitable gifts to numerous organizations; and Ben & Jerry's, maker of premium ice cream that supports a broad range of environmental, local grower and humanitarian causes.

The long tradition of social entrepreneurship seems to have always stemmed from a strong sense of dissatisfaction with the status quo – from people who not only believed that things could be better, but who also had ideas that could *make* them better. For us, that was certainly the case.

Perhaps this is why social entrepreneurship as a concept and business model has increased so dramatically over the last decade: We're increasingly disappointed by the inability of governments to solve problems, and we're disillusioned with the old business-as-usual principles that have led to corruption on Wall Street and, ultimately, the Great Recession and, possibly, the demise of American exceptionalism.

"Over the past decade, social entrepreneurship has gone from niche to mainstream," wrote Katherine Milligan of the Schwab Foundation in a Credit Suisse Research Institute report entitled *Investing for Impact*.

Milligan cites the following as evidence for this move to mainstream:

- The European Union recently launched its Social Business Initiative to spur growth in this sector.

- Several states in the United States, including California and New York, have passed legislation recognizing a special legal status for businesses with social missions (Benefit Corporation).

- The B Corporation status, conferred by B Lab as the certifying body, has been established to certify businesses "as having met a high standard of overall social and environmental performance, and as a result having access to a portfolio of services and support from B Lab" (from B Lab's website).

- There are roughly 200 social enterprises in the Schwab Foundation's network from 40 countries. The World Economic Forum launched a new community of "Global Shapers" in 2011, comprised of entrepreneurs and leaders in their 20s, organized into Hubs in more than 150 cities around the world. According to Mirjam Schöning, "Out of the group of 70 "Shapers" at Davos [site of the annual meeting of the World Economic Forum] this year, 40 percent of them claimed to be social entrepreneurs. That's how far we've come, where ten years ago we didn't even know what this was. Those who are now seen as the most active and brightest talents around the world are calling themselves social entrepreneurs."

- Investors have come to appreciate the social entrepreneurship business model, and a new kind of investment capital, called impact investment, has come to the fore. More than 200 impact investment funds have been registered in just the last few years. According to a 2011 article in *U.S. News & World Report* entitled "M.B.A. Programs Invest in Social Good," this investment sector is expected to grow to $500 billion by 2014.

The educational community has also come to embrace social entrepreneurship as a viable career path for business students. The nation's top business schools, including Harvard Business School, the Stanford Graduate School of Business, Cornell's Johnson Graduate School of Management, Northwestern's Kellogg School of Management, Duke's Fuqua School of Business, Yale's School of Management, and Oxford University's Saïd Business School have centers or programs for social entrepreneurship, social innovation, or social enterprise management.

In March 2012, journalist Kevin Roose of *The New York Times* reported, in his article entitled "Wall Street's Latest Campus Recruiting Crisis," that business students are increasingly uninterested in contributing their talents to large financial corporations, such as Goldman Sachs or JPMorgan Chase, which they have begun to view as corrupt or irresponsible in the wake of the recession and numerous corporate scandals. In 2008, 28 percent of Harvard's employed seniors went into finance; by 2011, that number had fallen to just 17 percent.

"Groups of protesters at Yale and Harvard stood outside bank recruiting sessions last fall, shouting slogans and holding signs with messages like 'Take a chance, don't go into finance,'" writes Roose.

Meanwhile, savvy business students are realizing that those financial giants, with their waves of layoffs and pay cuts, are no longer the best career prospects. They're turning to organizations like Net Impact that have cropped up to connect with world-changing ideas that they can put into practice on the job for non-profits, social enterprises, or corporations with corporate social responsibility initiatives.

Net Impact, a San Francisco-based 501(c)3 nonprofit with more than 300 volunteer-led chapters across the globe, is a community of more than 30,000 students, executives, social entrepreneurs, middle managers, and other change-makers who seek work that serves the triple-bottom line. "A small group of friends on several different business school campuses wanted to focus on more than just money-making, which was a radical concept for MBAs at the time," explains Net Impact's CEO, Liz Maw. "They believed the business skills they were developing could—and should—be used for more than simply generating shareholder profits; they should be used to generate a triple-bottom line supporting people, planet, *and* profit. They got together mostly to provide each other with support and ideas, faxed around an invitation to other campuses, and ended up with about 100 students also interested in socially responsible business at Georgetown University. This was the first Net Impact Conference."

Net Impact connects members through its local chapter events and its annual conference. It directs members to career opportunities with impact. Its student members hone business skills through its business plan competitions. And it brings members service opportunities to put their business skills to use to bring about social and environmental change in the workplace.

Net Impact's annual publication, *Business as UNusual*, which reviews graduate business programs offering impact-related coursework, reflects the shift in social consciousness; "the number of programs featured has grown a whopping 194 percent in the five years we've been publishing it (up from three dozen), which is a pretty significant indicator of how mainstream these issues are becoming for business-minded students," says Jess Sand, Net Impact's Senior Content Manager.

Another organization, ReWork, is similar in that it places young professionals directly into "disruptive, world-changing organizations," including nonprofits and social enterprises, where their work makes a real difference.

"I'd say 60 to 70 percent are people who feel like something is missing from their work," said Nathaniel Koloc, co-founder of ReWork, for a March 2012 article entitled "How To Find Meaningful Work" that ran on Co.Exist, Fast Company's social-consciousness-focused site.

"The conversations we have with people are very, very emotionally driven," said Koloc, "and I don't know that 10 years ago there were as many opportunities to fulfill these feelings, or how many companies had the balance of income, viability, meaning, and value of work."

It's true that the majority of people right now are unhappy at work. A Conference Board research group found that, in 2010, only 51 percent of the 5,000 workers surveyed found their jobs interesting, and only 45 percent were satisfied with their jobs – the lowest level ever recorded in the 22 years the study had been performed.

Consumers aren't happy with business as usual, either. In 2009, a *Huffington Post* article by Mitchell Markson titled "Social Purpose Becomes the New Social Status" reported that 70 percent of people "prefer to live in an eco-friendly house than merely a big house ... and that 68 percent feel it is becoming more unacceptable in their local community not to make efforts to show concern for their environment or to live a healthy lifestyle."

Sixty-four percent of people surveyed globally said they'd recommend brands that support good causes, and 63 percent "are looking to brands and companies to make it easier for them to make a difference."

"People today expect to be involved in positive social change," writes Markson, "and they expect the businesses they support with their increasingly hard-earned dollars to be involved as well. Where these expectations meet, something we haven't seen before is blossoming: a real, enduring partnership between people and brands that benefits both equally."

"It's interesting that, these days, young people really do have a social and environmental conscience, and in general don't want to be in businesses where they're contributing negatively," says Xavier Helgesen. "Social entrepreneurship is a way to get rich, create jobs, and do good. On the entrepreneur side, especially for young people, it's a sexy idea."

Jon Carson speculates that Social Capitalism really took off in the wake of 9-11. Carson, a serial entrepreneur, is the CEO and chairman of BiddingForGood.com, a charitable e-commerce company that connects fundraisers, cause-conscious shoppers, and socially responsible businesses through online auctions. BiddingForGood.com gets roughly a million visits per month to its shopping site, which makes it about three times the size of anybody else working in that space, including eBay, says Carson, adding that, with ten years under its belt, BiddingForGood.com has also been at it the longest.

With 20 years experience in building and scaling for-profit businesses that serve social purposes, Carson notes that social enterprises really saw marked growth post-9-11. "Cone Communications, an advertising agency that really invented the cause marketing company, did a survey with Roper that surveyed consumers. They asked, 'all things being equal, how likely are you to switch a brand to one that makes a contribution to a cause?' The beauty of it was that it was done every year, and the numbers pop in 2001, right after 9-11. Then it continues to slowly move upward."

What 9-11 did, says Carson, was show people how fragile the world is, and how short our time on this planet really is, thus the decision to make the most of our time by doing good. "The years since 2008 have really amplified that," says Carson. "There's now a sense that a number of things in our world aren't going very well. Whether you point to climate change indices, structural unemployment, the distribution of economic equality, the breakdown of the political system ... a bunch of systems are breaking down. People take that in at varying levels, but some segment of the population will respond and say they want to make the world better."

Jess Sand wrote an article for Net Impact entitled "Tracking the Rise of the Impact MBA," in which he cites the words of Lina Alfieri Stern, Director of the Levy-Rosenblum Institute for Entrepreneurship at Tulane University. Stern said, "With the unemployment situation, young people are growing up with the sense that companies aren't necessarily going to take care of them and they need to create their own opportunities ... So in large part, the rise in programming is driven by this bottom-up approach of students really expecting more... because of the internet, we're more connected to the rest of the world, more connected to other people's suffering, more connected to the problems that are intrinsic in our world. And students are looking for solutions to these problems."

More and more, he says, this is showing up in the Millennial generation, which surveys show have a higher tendency to seek a social mission in their work. "This generation grew up with 9-11, the economic downturn, and the Internet has always been in their lives. They're looking at the world differently, and they want more social impact in their world and have a much higher value on a work-family balance," says Carson.

Learning By Example

"The climate is ripe," wrote Jon Carson in a March 2012 column for *The Huffington Post,* "for social enterprises to be profitable while making great contributions toward social good." It's not simply a matter of people who are tired of waiting for solutions to come that aren't coming; it's also a matter of businesses doing what they can to stay afloat. Many businesses have sustained huge losses in the recession, while shifts in technology have changed the way people do business. The old ways don't work anymore, and being innovative is essential to survival. "Particularly in a post-recession economy, the successful businesses of the future will be those with a social mission built into their business model," Carson writes.

The man Kreece Fuchs and Xavier Helgesen credit as their mentor, David Murphy, Better World Books' former CEO, is now the Associate Dean of Entrepreneurship at the University of Notre Dame. His current duties include driving new thinking about entrepreneurship and innovation at the university, and looking for ways to spin intellectual property out of the school to make startups. He suggests that turning to business to solve social problems makes logical sense.

"The economy divides into three sections—nonprofits, the government, and the private sector," says Murphy. "The private sector is about two-thirds of that pie. So in the national debate, we hear about cuts and deficits, and with the largest social and environmental challenges we have, young people are saying, 'We just can't expect the government and nonprofits to fix it. They're strapped for cash and they can't always afford to have the best talent working for them.' So those people are saying, 'What about the private sector? They have the most money and the most talent, so why not direct solutions through that sector?'"

With that backdrop, it also helps to have witnessed a few successes, says Murphy. Companies like Patagonia and Starbucks, Tom's Shoes, Grameen Bank, Better World Books and B Lab now stand as examples of what can be done by the private sector. And for many aspiring social entrepreneurs, there's also a steadily growing cadre of mentors out there familiar with the Social Capitalist model for business and the growing body of resources out there to support that model.

We know that for us, having had great mentors of our own in those first days of planning our business—Spencer in the addiction recovery realm (and in staying sober), Josh's father in the drive and work ethic to keep pushing forward no matter what, and Robert Kiyosaki in the realm of financial education—made taking our next steps doable. They showed us examples of what was possible, and what could be accomplished with a clear head, strong work ethic, and knowledge about income, expenses, assets, and liabilities. And they became our first in a series of teachers whose instruction and words of support became critical to our success.

Chapter Thought

The government was not designed to financially support people. Governments were designed to create laws that protect entrepreneurs. Businesses are designed to provide jobs, goods, and services, which contribute to the GDP and provide value to humanity and the economy.

Chapter Four

When the Student is Ready, the Teacher Appears

"Social entrepreneurs are not content just to give a fish or teach how to fish. They will not rest until they have revolutionized the fishing industry."

—Bill Drayton, CEO, and founder of Ashoka Innovators

In 2007, Michael Holthouse's 10-year-old daughter, Lissa, asked him if she could have a pet turtle. Because she already owned multiple pets, Holthouse quickly responded with a sound "no." The next day, Lissa, taking a cue from her entrepreneurial father, asked if she could set up a lemonade stand. Unbeknownst to Holthouse, the lemonade stand had a direct correlation to the desired turtle; Lissa had decided she was going to use her profits from her lemonade stand to buy the turtle for herself. This experience sparked an idea in Holthouse's head: to use this simple American childhood pastime as a way to teach entrepreneurship to youth across the country.

Holthouse, a successful entrepreneur who had just ten years prior become a multimillionaire when he sold his computer network services company to Sprint, had spent a year of his life looking at ways to give back by exploring different programs that targeted at-risk kids. He traveled the country interacting with different organizations, asking questions of organizational leaders, and evaluating a variety of environmental factors.

From that experience, he developed Prepared 4 Life, his nonprofit that ran numerous after-school programs for youth.

"Here I was, a reasonably accomplished entrepreneur, and I'd never taken the time to teach my daughter how free enterprise works," recalls Holthouse. "It was an 'a-ha moment' that this was something that could have an extraordinary impact on millions of youth."

Which is just what it did. After Lissa set up her lemonade stand with a friend, with her father's guidance, and made enough money to buy her turtle, Prepared 4 Life rolled out Lemonade Day, a free, fun, experiential learning program that teaches youth how to start, own, and operate a business—in this case, a lemonade stand. On Lemonade Day, an entire communities of kids are encouraged to set up lemonade stands and glean valuable lessons about entrepreneurship. The first Lemonade Day in 2007 was in Houston, Texas, and by 2011 there were more than 30 cities across North America taking part.

When our kids want something, we always ask them, "How are you going to create that?" It gets their creativeness in action. Rather than always buying or giving them what they want, asking them that question keeps them in the entrepreneurial mindset. They are always looking to give so that they can receive more, start some form of "business" or sell items they have created.

It just goes to show that you're never too old or too experienced to learn or try something new. And all around us there are teachers (and they may even be our kids!) who are ready to share valuable lessons with us whenever we're ready to listen to them.

Willing Students

Timing, as they say, is everything. Any other day, we might have added Robert Kiyosaki's audiobook to the growing pile of off-the-wall, discarded gifts from my dad. But on that day in December 2001, we received the lessons we needed exactly when we deserved to hear them. Here was a well-respected leader in the business world, a self-made man who himself had also not done well in school. As a kid, he had also had teachers label him as stupid. Yet he had found remarkable success following his own path, and on those CDs we heard him saying in so many words that we didn't have to follow the predetermined path, either.

In fact, we heard him giving us permission—no, outright *urging* us—to take a different path than everyone else in order to find our own success. We heard him saying that it was lifelong learning, not book-learning or the grades we had gotten on tests, that would determine our success. We heard him say we had the choice. It wasn't about following a certain path, but choosing our *own* path. Are you following your own path, or someone else's?

One of the things Robert said that really stuck with us was this: "The reason most people don't get anywhere in life is because they are afraid to fail." Failure is how we learn, he says, and the sooner you fail, the faster your progress toward success.

Like we said, on any other day, that lesson might not have meant anything to us. But on this day, we heard him telling us that not only could we be successful blazing a new trail, but that failure wasn't even something to be afraid of. And as it often does with the words of our most valuable teachers, his words came at *exactly* the time when we were supposed to hear them. It was like he was talking directly to us.

So here we were with an idea; we had a mountain of research; we had the support of Spencer, an expert and practitioner in the field who had spoken those magic words to me in rehab that generated our business idea; we had the incredible words of guidance from Robert Kiyosaki that inspired us and became the catalyst for our life reinvention; and, thanks to Spencer, we had a virtual how-to manual for how to meet all the licensing requirements for our first rehabilitation center. But more than that, we both knew at a core level that we could do this, and that everything in our lives had led to this moment.

Which brings us to one of the most important pieces of advice we can share with you: Always seek the insights and wisdom of teachers. They will come into your life when they're meant to, and if your eyes and ears are truly open and you ask the right questions, they will teach you the things you are ready to know.

You don't have to be a particularly religious or spiritual person to believe this concept. Just consider the example of a new car.

Say you're out shopping for a new car, and while browsing a lot, one car catches your eye. This may not be a car you ever thought about before, and you may have never looked at one twice. But today you did. The more you think about this car—its color, its price, its size—the more it seems to be the right fit for you.

So you go home to think about the cars you saw that day, and on the drive home, you pass four of them. In fact, the next morning, when you're driving to work, you see three more. All of a sudden, you see this car everywhere. You go to work and start talking about your car-shopping experience, and a coworker tells you that she owns that same make and model of car, only a year older. Or maybe her husband or sister has one. Now you can ask questions and learn a bit about what it's like to own this car, and whether he or she is happy with it.

Our point here is that when we're receptive to learning something, the lesson comes to us. When you ask the right questions and come from a place of openness, you will begin to see abundance that has always been there. And as an entrepreneur, it's crucial that you remain open at all times to the lessons that can come your way from unexpected places, not just when you're starting out but *always*. There's always more to learn.

In a lot of ways, we started behaving like the lead character of *Forrest Gump,* Tom Hanks' simple-minded man who makes his way through life and into many of the most memorable moments in history by just putting one

Even look at the teachers and those around you that have discouraged you, what lessons can you learn from them, what have they said you couldn't do? Did you let that stop you or drive you? We can learn from everyone we come in contact with if we are open to it. And while we may not seek out these teachers to be mentors, be open to the possibility that you can learn something.

foot in front of the other, following his own gut and the wise words of trusted friends. We started doing the same thing. We asked people we respected, "What would the next step be?" or, "How did you do that?" They'd tell us their experiences and we'd follow their advice, just like Forrest Gump.

Sure, it seems ridiculously simple, but sometimes the most powerful lessons really are that simple. It's how we embarked upon our financial education, too. We were amazed at how many successful people were willing to give us their time and knowledge to assist us when we had questions. When Forrest Gump received advice, he said, in his southern drawl, "Okaaaay," and that's pretty much what we did when people we respected would provide us with advice, too. In the martial arts, I was taught that the best way to honor your instructor was to truly listen and apply the principles you learn. Simply put, that's what we did. We managed our fears and went to work, one day at a time, one step at a time.

It's important to note that the word "respect" is key here. When it comes to professional mentors, we looked for people with success in the area in question. We consulted people with proven experience, and not just opinions to spare. A major mistake people often make is by asking the wrong person for advice. We would not ask a three-time divorced individual for marriage advice, or an employee about becoming an entrepreneur. Choose your advisors carefully.

So when Spencer said "Go to Florida," or when Robert said, "You have to shift your context of thinking," we said, "Okay!" Because we respected what they had achieved in their fields, and then we went out and did it. It was really that simple. We were willing to accept the potential of falling flat on our faces, because:

1. We felt we had nothing to lose at this point.

2. Failure is one way you learn (remember?).

3. Our teachers had been there and done that—they were real-world instructors.

Even when the advice of others didn't always pan out for us, that was okay, too. Because through those attempts, we learned what *didn't* work, which is just as important, and that eventually assisted us with finding our way. Listening to others' advice also opened our eyes to possibilities we may not have thought of, or opened our awareness to new ways of doing things. The more we became aware, the more solutions we came up with.

And here's another reason to seek advisors: If nothing else, it's important to have someone to support our dreams, no matter how outlandish they may seem to others. "It's reassuring to know you're not crazy!" says Chris Hershey, who even with her years of experience not only still seeks mentors herself, but is now in the position to give back by mentoring others just starting out in business. "Some people still look at me like, 'What are you *doing*? You're out of your mind! You could be making a lot more money!' So it's nice to have company. I still have a few mentors, senior folks and colleagues who encourage me when I need it."

Kreece Fuchs and Xavier Helgesen credit much of their success to the mentorship they received from David Murphy early on. "To have someone experienced who understands aspects of cash flow and banking, it was invaluable, and we certainly wouldn't be where we are today without David Murphy," says Fuchs, adding that Murphy was one of several mentors and advisors over the years, including Jeff Kurtzman, who provided valuable insights into drafting the first business plan for Better World Books.

"One of the dumbest things we did early on was not find mentors, or people we respected at the university or through other channels," says Helgesen. "I think a lot of people think that things are different now because of the Internet, and they can get what they need that way. But a few good mentors are just invaluable."

"Mentors have been key in managing teams. And you've got to find someone to work through issues with, to bounce ideas off of, and we've had that from the get-go with David and that's expanded to a number of people. It's important that they aren't people you're reporting to as well, so you can be more open with concerns, especially with sensitive issues, who will give you frank advice."

Finding Dollars and Sense

Lisa and I certainly required some frank advice. We had a lot to learn about opening a business and raising capital, and it took hearing some tough criticism from another teacher in order to learn it.

Because with all the things we had going for us, what we didn't have was a place to create this business. Because of the *Rich Dad* teachings about passive income and the numerous tax benefits, we knew we wanted to purchase a property rather than lease one. But to do this, we had to have money, which we also didn't have. After ten years of life-challenging hard work in the nightclubs and with the police department, our total assets basically amounted to $30,000 in a money market account and our home (which, as we knew from Robert Kiyosaki, isn't really an asset).

We both realized that the success of any business depended on an understanding of money—how it works, how it flows, how to manage it, how to respect it, and how to grow it. We knew that we'd need money to market our business to draw clients. We knew we would have to make payroll, cover the legal costs that were inherent in this field, and we would, of course, require money to live on and grow our fledgling business. As nice as it would have been to rely on the goodness of volunteers, we knew that the best counselors, even those with the biggest of hearts, would eventually require payment if we wanted them to stick around.

We also realized that no matter how successful we were in our new business, if we didn't know the language of money, we'd never fully achieve our mission to build a global world-class healing program and reach true freedom.

When I went to dinner with my dad to share news of our plan with him, he was, of course, thrilled to hear that the gift he had given us had been so influential. I shared with him our hopes for the drug and alcohol rehabilitation center, and the story of Spencer's invaluable mentorship, which had included inviting us to Florida, opening his doors and his resources to us, answering a barrage of questions, and providing us with his precious time and materials.

I held my breath as I attempted to read his expression (Would he lunge across the table to wring my neck? Would he laugh and say we were both out of our minds?), but he only looked at me with only frank sincerity and said, "Son, whatever I can do to support you, let me know, okay?"

I didn't expect anything from him. His acceptance meant the world to us, and we truly thought it was enough. But when we put him to the test months later, we learned that he truly did mean what he'd said.

There's a legend that when explorer Hernán Cortés and his crew landed on the shores of Mexico in 1519, he was heard shouting, "Burn the ships!" He ordered the ships burned in order to remove the temptation to retreat and go home rather than plunging into the unknown.

Well, we definitely burned our ships.

It had begun when we arrived home from rehab, and I saw that Lisa had gotten rid of all the liquor-branded mirrors, glassware, coasters, and shot glasses. She had filled garbage bags with these items and more—t-shirts, hats, all kinds of swag handed out by liquor companies with deep pockets looking to provide us with incentive to push their products on customers. Lisa and I saw these things as a kind of poison, so all of it was thrown away. Our home became our sanctuary, and all the reminders of partying were gone (except, for the time being, my work shirts, which I would still wear for my work at the nightclub).

Having broken the news to my surprisingly supportive father, Lisa and I began immediately working toward extracting ourselves from the nightclub, and I was finally able to walk away from the family business on October 15, 2002. My focus, finally, could be exclusively on developing the first Journey Center, and I often devoted 18-hour days to it. Lisa remained at the police department, never letting on that we were working on our own business, and her salary covered our basic living expenses, which meant she would stay there until we felt the business was well underway. Despite the exhaustion of pregnancy, she would work from 6 p.m. to 6 a.m., a twelve-hour shift, each day and then come home and work on the business with me. Her days off were completely focused on our new business. We worked as a team and dedicated ourselves to this new mission.

And we were broke, getting broker every day. Failure loomed large before us before we had even started. But we had burned our ships—there was no going back, no matter what. It would literally have been, for us, a life-and-death situation.

We crunched numbers and realized that, if we were really cautious and saved up enough to make a down payment on a property in which to house our rehab center, we could probably get started in about 25 years. The wind had been sucked out of our sails.

"What would Robert do?" became our steady refrain, and we found ourselves returning to the CDs and our copious notes, until we came upon the three *Rich Dad* principles that would see us through:

> We used the Rich Dad principle of keep your day job and start a part time business. Except we started a full time business while I kept my day job. And while it was a tough year until I did quit my job, it was well worth the dedication to our new mission. Most entrepreneurs work long hours for the reward and success that can be achieved.

1. Divide to Multiply
2. Work for Free
3. Use Other People's Money (OPM)

Following this advice, we made a plan to get our own financial house in order, and that starts with paying ourselves first. Knowing that it was too easy, and too tempting, to spend money if the bulk of what we had was in one account, we realized the value of creating separate bank accounts, and even before I had quit my job, we began a plan involving the strategic use of three piles of money:

- Reserve
- Investments
- Donations

The genius of this plan became even clearer to us when we had only one income. Every time Lisa got paid, we took her paycheck to the bank and cashed it, and then we put a few dollars in each pile. The rest paid bills. If we had spare change, we put it in a new fourth pile, which we called "Fun Money," and which occasionally allowed us to treat ourselves to something fun. We made no credit card purchases unless we intended to pay the bill in full each month.

After a while, we had enough in each pile to start new accounts. We called them:

- Necessities (for bills)
- Investing (for buying assets)
- Reserve (savings)
- Donation (tithing)
- Fun
- Kids (future)
- Taxes

This system enabled us to take control of our money—if the cash wasn't in the account, we didn't spend it. Every dollar earned was divided using percentages among the accounts. By using percentages, this allowed us to create goals and measure the progress.

We followed the principle "divide to multiply" to create this strategy, which we called our Plan to Be Secure (PBS) System, and though it took a great investment of discipline, time, and patience, it did provide us with a foundation of security. At the time, our living expenses comprised 83% of our income. Today they only comprise 32% (55% of our income now goes into our investment account). By dividing our bank accounts, we were able to multiply the balances.

We were and continue to be diligent in this process every month. It assists us in creating the lifestyle we want and the discipline necessary to create that freedom.

Chapter Thought

Do you have a plan in place that's similar to this? What could you do today to implement a strategy like this?

So prior to even considering how we were going to use other people's money to finance our dream, we were well on the way to having our own finances in order. After all, if we couldn't take care of our own money, how could we ask to take care of someone else's? We didn't have much money at the time, but we had gained a new sense of responsible stewardship for the money we had. That was crucial in maintaining our integrity, which would be essential in finding the money to make our dream come true.

We believed we were now ready to approach a bank and seek a business loan. We felt confident about our financial picture, which demonstrate stability, and we had solid research about the addiction treatment industry and our target market, which we spent a few days compiling into business plan several pages long, and which we believed was solid enough to get us started and compensate for our lack of cash, credit, and collateral. Surely, we thought, once the loan officer sees our passion, our new understanding of assets and liabilities, and our extensive research, that would seal the deal!

Yeah, right. We were in for a new learning experience.

Cautiously optimistic, we dressed in our very best clothes and entered the bank, plan in hand, and asked to speak to a loan officer. Despite our attempts at small talk, the loan officer asked us two very direct questions: Where did we go to college, and was one of us a treatment counselor?

Having digested the fact that neither of us had any formal training in the field and that our professional experience consisted of nightclub work and law enforcement, he moved on to the clarification of our assets—the $30K in a money market.

He condescendingly referred us to the Small Business Administration's loan program, apologized that there was nothing else he could do for us, and bid us good day.

We were disheartened, frustrated, and angry at the bank and at ourselves. We retooled our plan and our pitch over and over, and then visited bank after bank, hoping to find one that would take a chance on us. None did. We filled out the SBA paperwork, thinking that maybe that really was the best course of action. But because their paperwork required the same kinds of information that the banks had requested—information that didn't put us in a favorable light as far as they were concerned, we got nowhere with that, either.

With each rejection, though, we got savvier. We learned the language that banks used and wanted to hear from us. We got feedback from them about what looked questionable in terms of our target market or our financial plan. Failure can be a merciless teacher, but a teacher it most definitely is.

After visiting countless banks, filling out books of paperwork, and repeatedly being denied, we admitted defeat by the banking industry and thought about going after grant money from private or foundational donors. We felt that surely there must be a person or organization that provided funding to minority women or to citizens of Vietnamese origin. But what we found was that these sources had strings attached that contradicted our desire for freedom.

Asking our families wasn't really an option—Lisa's mother would surely balk at a plan that eradicated the security of her government job, and few of our relatives

It was a good process to go through, not necessarily a fun one but it gave us practice talking the talk and learning to be better. Not to mention we also had some fun by taking our house off the asset column (bankers version) and telling them we don't consider it an asset. We said it was their asset, not ours. Obviously they didn't like that but we knew we would be denied so we learned to have fun while failing and practicing.

had anywhere near the kind of money we would need to purchase a decent property.

It was time to ask my father for some advice. After all, he started with nothing and over the years successfully raised capital to fund his many nightclubs; he was our expert. I decided to take dad up on his offer and ask for some help.

He didn't offer us money, and we didn't ask for it. Instead, I asked him to meet me for dinner, where I shared our frustrations over what had happened with the banks, and our lack of funding—even a lack of interest—from anyone with money to loan. "I feel like they're laughing at us," I told him.

After pointing out that maybe the banks actually *were* laughing at our lack of financial or business experience, he considered for a moment and then suggested that he introduced us to a "private wealthy" that he knew—an accredited investor with personal money willing to invest in certain promising enterprises.

Absolutely, we said, and asked my dad to arrange a meeting.

A few days later, he called us to say that Arvis, his "private wealthy" friend, would meet with me at 5 p.m. the following day. "Bring your business plan," he said.

Gulp. A professional *business plan?*

We had no such thing—not a real one, anyway. What we'd given the banks had been a rudimentary listing of statistical data and a brief description of the business we planned to start, most of which we'd scrapped after our colossal failure at getting anywhere with the banks.

Using our dial-up Internet connection, we scoured the Web for "how to write a business plan," and found a lot of complicated resources that wouldn't work for our purposes of drafting a real plan in 24 hours. Showing the banks the plan was one thing, but the idea of showing it to a wealthy investor put additional pressure on us. We could see our inexperience, and it was our job to put a great plan together. Online, we found one that was less complicated, selected that as our model, and settled in for an all-night session of business plan writing.

It took 15 attempts to arrive at a version we were content with, then a rush job at the local 24-hour office store to print and bind the document, but we had a business plan we actually really liked to hand over to Arvis when I would meet him in Boulder City that evening. We had decided that I would go alone with my father to the first meeting, since my dad had a relationship with him and it would keep things simpler. Lisa would stay home and continue to work on locations and property.

> It's always good to have someone who can review and give you an honest opinion about your business plan before you present it to potential investors, partners, etc. In reality, it was more like our 200th plan but 15 official attempts.

"Arvis is elderly, so be patient with him, okay? He's in his 80s," my dad instructed me when he picked me up to take me to meet Arvis.

I assured him that I would, of course, be respectful and patient with this man who was kind enough to meet with us on such short notice. But I became skeptical when we pulled into a mobile home park. Surely this couldn't be right. What was a "private wealthy" (an accredited investor) doing living here? At the time I didn't know that Arvis was the owner of the entire mobile home park, in addition to several others, some shopping centers, and a few storage units in Nevada and Arizona.

Arvis greeted us at the door in a blue baseball cap, and welcomed us into his "office"—a kitchen table covered in paperwork. We could feel Arvis sizing us up as I walked into the trailer.

"So, you want money, huh?" he asked me, bypassing any small talk or niceties.

"Yes, sir," I said, watching him squint to see me better.

"How much do you want?" he asked.

He had stumped me already. In all our planning, all our research, all the times we'd gone to banks to ask for money, and even in our overnight business plan cram session, we had neglected to ask ourselves this one fundamental question: How much money should we ask for? I could have thrown a number out there, but who knew whether it was too much or too little, and there was no support for it... In less than a minute, Arvis had sucked the wind from our sails. *Wow*, I thought, *he's a pro*. I realized then that, regardless of his advanced age, he was probably as sharp as he'd ever been at such negotiations.

Dumbfounded and tongue-tied, the only thing I could think to do was hand him my business plan. He took it from me, sat down in his 1930s-era metal chair with an ugly yellow-and-white-checkered plastic seat pad, flipped through a few pages of the plan, and tossed it back at me. "Son, this plan sucks," he said. "Get out of here." I looked to my dad—*was this a joke?*—and saw his nod. No, this was no joke. I was being asked to leave.

I left the trailer alone, and stood outside the mobile home feeling humiliated and dejected for the longest 20 minutes of my life.

Finally, my dad emerged and marched silently to the car. We both got in and sat there wordlessly as he pulled out of the mobile home park and headed us toward home. Eventually, he spoke.

"So what did you learn?" he asked me.

I had learned that Arvis was a real jerk, I said, piling excuses and justifications upon each other, pointing fingers at Arvis and anyone else who didn't see the genius behind what Lisa and I intended to do with our business. Didn't anyone understand that we were going to *saves lives and bring families back together again*?

"Welcome to the real world," he told me, chuckling at my anger. "So, now, what do you plan to do about it?"

At that moment, all I wanted to do was go home and fume some more. When I arrived home and Lisa greeted me, more and more anger poured out of me. Who the hell did that guy think he was, talking to me like that?

But as I talked, spewing anger at the unfairness of it all, I found myself expressing anger *at myself*. Arvis had been right. We hadn't been prepared. We had put the basics of the plan together at the last minute and based on an Internet template. He was just telling the honest truth. The plan did suck. And if we couldn't take the time to write a decent business plan, who did we think we were kidding? How could we convince anyone we were serious about this?

A few days later, after things had cooled off, Lisa and I went back to the drawing board and rewrote the plan. I asked my dad humbly if he could arrange another meeting with Arvis, and in the month and a half it took to secure one, we continued working on the plan, perfecting it. We scoped out more properties in which to house our treatment center, to sustain our momentum and develop a more concrete plan. We wouldn't let Arvis, or anyone for that matter, slow us down.

We'd quickly realized that establishing a rehab in Las Vegas was a little like holding a Weight Watchers meeting at a doughnut shop. After all, who in their right mind would come to Vegas to get sober? If it were their first time in Vegas, with all its lights and glamour, we would lose them at the airport. That meant that the center would only serve a local market, and we knew that our first center was to have international guests. We didn't want to limit our admissions to a locals-only market. We began looking at neighboring states, determining what would be the best location for such a business. California, with its out-of-sight real estate prices and oversaturation of rehab and treatment centers didn't make sense for us. But Colorado and Utah both seemed appealing.

Then we discovered this fact: Utah has the highest rate of prescription drug abuse and the second-highest rate of methamphetamine abuse in the country. Plus, at the time, it was greatly underserved by private adult treatment resources. The zoning laws and real estate market looked favorable.

All our sights were set on Utah, and after scouring roughly 150 available properties, and walking through at least 20 of them, we identified a bed and breakfast property in Salt Lake City that had closed after the 2002 Winter Olympics. The owners wanted to sell it lock, stock, and barrel, furniture and all. It was a perfect turnkey property for us. It was simply too good a deal to pass up, so we made an offer without any money in hand.

That's how we learned that once a deal was secured, raising money was much easier because we would have something tangible riding on the loan. It carried more pressure, but it also called for more determination from us to raise capital more quickly. We revised the business plan to reflect a concrete amount of money, the purchase price, and prepared, very confidently, to meet Arvis with our updated plan.

My dad and I meet with him at the old Showboat Casino in Las Vegas. Arvis looked at the fish of the day and asked about the market place. The server told him it was $23.99.

> *Once you get past the emotions of failing, like we did, you can learn many lessons. There are always valuable lessons to learn that can make you more successful each time.*

"No, no, that's too much," he said, and ordered soup, despite my insistence that he should order what he wanted, because it was my treat. He refused. Again, we were off to a great start.

We quickly got down to business. I handed Arvis the revised plan. "You know how much money you want this time?" he asked, skeptically opening the plan.

"Yes, I do," I said, glad to have a viable response for once. "I'm asking for $1.5 million, which will be secured by the property in Salt Lake City," I explained, pointing to the pictures I'd included with the plan.

After a few moments, he closed the plan, set it aside, and changed topics. Dinner arrived, and we ate and made small talk. I was afraid we'd get all the way through dinner without discussing the reason for our meeting, and once we had eaten all our dinners, I could no longer take the suspense. "So, what about the plan?" I asked.

"I'll take a look and get back to you," he said, making it clear that I shouldn't push my luck.

I backed off.

I called my dad each and every day, asking, "Well? Have you heard anything?" No word came from Arvis. Then, nearly two weeks after our meeting, my dad called to report that, unfortunately, Arvis had declined our request. It seemed that our plan still had not passed his test. "Are you *sure* you guys really want to do this?" my dad pressed, reminding us of the stress of running a business, the sacrifices we would have to make, the irritations of working with a team of employees.

Yes, we insisted, heartbroken. This is what we *really* wanted. How could there be any doubt? We'd given our bodies and souls to this plan!

"It's just, well, that plan really is bad," he told us.

The joy we had felt over the acceptance of our offer on the property was supplanted with devastation, like a punch in the gut. We were now tied up in a property we couldn't afford, for a business we didn't have.

Lisa and I had talked late into the night about what we would do. We had burned all our ships—we couldn't go back now, nor did we want to. All we could do was plow forward. We looked through the plan with critical eyes and determined that yes, indeed, our plan had too many holes.

We worked some more on it. We consulted expert resources, we read more *Rich Dad* materials, and we sealed up every hole we could find until we felt we were ready for another shot, if Arvis would give us one.

I called my dad, he lined up the meeting, and this time Lisa joined us. I felt confident that my partner was with me, and I fully intended to ask Arvis for the reasons why he had declined our plan. This time, I would fight to be heard.

We returned to the mobile home and joined Arvis at the kitchen table. Arvis probed us about why we wanted to start such a business. In the course of an hour, we shared our story with him honestly, and revealed our full commitment to the venture. We shared with him the pains and fears of addiction and what we had gone through together. We told Arvis our story and why Journey meant so much to us. And, miraculously, he seemed genuinely interested. This wasn't a sales pitch, this was our story, from the heart.

When we'd finished, he sat back in his chair, looked us both in the eye, and said, "I can see now why you want to start this business. You're stubborn. You didn't give up when I repeatedly declined your plan. And in business, people

Until one is committed, there is an easier chance to quit or back out. Making a tangible commitment, such as securing a property before having the funding, strengthens the commitment and determination to see it through. Look at other places where you can make a commitment to assist you in reaching your goals.

are going to beat you up and knock you down. You didn't give up. And you *must* keep coming back. That's what it takes to be successful. Because of that, I'll loan you the money. I'm in."

So with our hearts and souls, my father's assistance, and a business plan (thanks to Arvis), we had our $1.5 million.

We had locked up the property with the bed and breakfast included for $1,275,000, and could put the $225K that remained into startup capital. We were in the game!

And that's really what great teachers do: They push us to do more and be better when we don't believe we have anything left to give. They tell us what we need to hear exactly when we need to hear it, even if we don't always like what they have to say. They assist us in becoming the best, highest versions of ourselves, even if that means that sometimes they have to tear us down to get us up there.

Entrepreneurship Is a Team Sport

TechnoServe is a nonprofit organization founded in 1968 by businessman and philanthropist Ed Bullard to aid rural people in developing countries harness the power of private enterprise to lift themselves out of poverty. It does this in a number of ways—working with stakeholders to develop and strengthen plans and production, providing entrepreneurship and business training in the classroom, and holding business plan competitions (BPCs) that enable applicants to receive assistance and education while offering opportunities to win seed money. TechnoServe also pairs struggling entrepreneurs with willing business leaders to encourage a mentorship relationship.

According to a 2009 Business Plan Competitions Study by TechnoServe, to evaluate the impact of BPCs in terms of those entrepreneurs' success, participants in the competitions were nearly twice as likely to survive two years, and generated 2.5 times the two-year sales growth of non-participants. "Receiving personal feedback on their business plans from well-respected local entrepreneurs validated their ideas and ambitions, and boosted their confidence and motivation," says the report.

In fact, those participants without "aftercare," or continued involvement from TechnoServe mentors, felt that even limited support from business experts would have been extremely helpful in overcoming challenges.

"The role of mentorship is so important," says TechnoServe President and CEO Bruce McNamer, explaining that in terms of the BPCs, a number of critical factors determine success. "One of the most critical success factors is an ongoing relationship with someone who knows entrepreneurs and plays a sounding board, even in their mentoring role post-competition ... They can be a bridge to useful service providers, vendors, or contacts, and they're someone to give advice on managing and running an enterprise in general."

Mirjam Schöning seconds this. The peer exchange benefits offered through the Schwab Foundation has become an unexpected value of membership, she says. "It's something we didn't necessarily realize when we started. But several hundred conferences later, I still hear it's the most important value in the field. The exchange is extremely important."

"My counsel is to try to find a mentor as early as you can, if you're serious," says David Murphy at Notre Dame. "I think it's absolutely key. In many ways, it's more important than the social mission or goal itself."

He adds that while many people only seek mentors in order to secure capital, mentors offer value that money simply can't buy. "Mentors are so helpful in terms of making sure you're paying attention to the model, getting in front of customers, and giving great advice on capitalizing on advice," Murphy says. Business plan competitions in general, he says, are great spots for finding mentors; after all, it was how he had connected with Better World Books. Fellow university alumni and college accelerator programs are also great spots for making mentorship connections.

"Really good mentors aren't in it, especially in the beginning, for the money," Murphy says. "They shouldn't be demanding equity, but they should be interested in helping to get the enterprise off the ground. Then, if it's going to be more serious, it's a different game... maybe you hire them, give them equity or a board position. But it's still probably the best money you can spend."

Plus, mentors often gain a lot from the exchange, too, says Michael Holthouse as he reflects on the experience of guiding his daughter in her lemonade stand. "One of the greatest ways to learn anything is to attempt to teach it to others," he says.

Holthouse suggests that the Young Presidents' Organization (YPO) of which Lisa and I are members, the Entrepreneurs' Organization (EO), the World Presidents' Organization, and many other professional associations are wonderful places to connect with advisors, peers and mentors. And it's a crucial thing, considering the nature of entrepreneurship.

"Every single journey that an entrepreneur goes down is unique, in its time, in its industry, in its economic environment, in the products and services it's trying to provide says Michael Holthouse. "Entrepreneurship is experiential. I'm not suggesting that it's not beneficial to go to a school like Babson or any one of the other business school or school of entrepreneurship. They're helpful tools. But what entrepreneurs excel at is taking learning and applying it to situations to produce outcomes that are extraordinary. So oftentimes, you'll find entrepreneurs will gather around others in order to be able to share life experiences... so they don't have to make all the mistakes themselves but learn from others how not to make them."

Having a mentor can also assist in minimizing failures and mistakes. They have been there, done that and while you will still make mistakes, they may not be as harsh.

Chapter Thought

If you are committed to a vision, don't let the word "no" get in your way. Often, it is just about getting to the one person who will say "yes." Know that you will be told no, and be open to the process. Have a scorecard that counts the number of times that a person or your intuition says no to you or your business plan. Keep going until you hear "yes." For each no, write down what you learned, and what you'll do differently next time. Regroup, make the corrections, and go back in for another round. Get your YES!

Chapter Five

Building a Business Around the Heart (Your "Why")

"[T]here is nothing more difficult to carry out, nor more doubtful of success, nor more dangerous to handle, than to initiate a new order of things."

—Niccolò Machiavelli, *The Prince*

In 1974, Bangladesh was experiencing severe famine that resulted in the deaths of thousands of people. At the time, Muhammad Yunus was an economics teacher at a Chittagong University in southern Bangladesh. All around him, emaciated, hungry people flooded the streets of the capital, Dhaka, looking for help. "Often they sat so still that one could not be sure whether they were alive or dead," said Yunus in *Banker to the Poor,* the book he co-authored with Alan Jolis.

Though gainfully employed and passionate about the economic principles that he espoused to students, he could no longer find joy in the work in light of the crushing misery that surrounded him. "How could I go on telling my students make believe stories in the name of economics?" Yunus writes. "I needed to run away from these theories and from my textbooks and discover the real-life economics of a poor person's existence."

And that's exactly what he did, in the nearby village of Jobra. Yunus' blog describes how, in Jobra, he witnessed "how the loan sharks enslaved the villagers." Using what he'd observed and collaborating with his students, he formulated several ideas to be of real help. The one that seemed most helpful was an idea for providing micro-loans to entrepreneurs, to free the villagers from the grasp of these loan sharks. In his blog, Yunus writes:

> With my students, I was able to help the women in a small way. Acting as the guarantor, I was able to arrange loans from the bank for the poor people of the village. Alongside the loans, I added a savings program. At that time, women in the village did not have the capacity to save. The savings program started with 25 paisa in savings per week. Today the total amount of savings by the borrowers stands at 6 billion Taka!

Grameen (in Bengali, "rural" or "villager") Bank was born, and Yunus found his life's calling—giving villagers, mostly women, a hand up out of poverty; currently 96 percent of borrowers are women. Membership in the Grameen Bank grew (95 percent of the equity ownership of the bank are borrowers, with the remaining 5 percent being government-owned), and Yunus' work went beyond the financial as he worked with illiterate members to teach them to write their names in the dirt with sticks.

Grameen Bank revolutionized the banking industry, turning all prior notions of bank loans on their heads with its policy of only loaning to the very poorest of people—to qualify for a loan, village women must demonstrate that they and their families own *less* than one-half acre of land—and doing away with collateral requirements.

Being in an industry that empowers others to take control of their lives is what Social Entrepreneurism and Social Capitalism is all about. Giving people the choices to build their own freedom and make a difference is one way we will change the world.

The idea spread. As of this writing, there are 2,565 branches of Grameen Bank worldwide, working with people in more than 81,000 villages in approximately 100 countries. It has earned a profit nearly every year since its inception. And in October 2006, Grameen Bank and Muhammad Yunus jointly earned the Nobel Peace Prize.

"Lasting peace cannot be achieved unless large population groups find ways in which to break out of poverty," wrote the Norwegian Nobel Committee in its award statement. "Micro-credit is one such means. Development from below also serves to advance democracy and human rights."

Three decades after Yunus began his project, Grameen Bank is considered the preeminent social enterprise, and it has been called the single most important third-world development of the last century.

And all because one man wanted to once again believe in what he was teaching.

Why You Must Have a "Why"

Research shows that Social Capitalists have one thing in common: A deep and abiding natural passion for solving problems. As we said early on in this book, passion is everything for Social Capitalists. It's the thing that gets you out of bed, and that pushes you forward when there's little promise of success. Whatever your passion, your "why," your calling, it's incredibly important that you know your why and have one, because without it, all you have is a job.

What characterizes social entrepreneurs isn't all that different from what distinguishes any entrepreneur—a willingness to take risks, commitment to an ideal, and a passionate commitment to solving a problem. Usually that comes from a deeply personal, transformative event or experience that drives that idea or business.

That's the essential piece of the puzzle, too, in terms of accomplishing the necessary, sometimes unpleasant or mundane tasks of running a business. "Social capitalists have to be salespeople. They can't be bashful fundraisers. They don't spend time walking the fields with farmers in Africa, helping them to get out of poverty, which is probably why they started in the first place. Rather, they raise money, establish the foundations of the business, and spend their time convincing people of the merits of that business.

In our case, Journey Healing Centers may have stemmed from our personal experience with addiction, our commitment to forming a mission-driven rehab center that treats people with dignity and respect, as well as to free others from the shackles of addiction. But as we had begun to learn, the day-to-day experience of building the business didn't put us on those front lines, experiencing the joys of hands-on work with our guests. We weren't walking our fields, either.

Though neither of us intended to become a licensed counselor, it was the creation of this business model that drove us forward each day, despite the fact that we weren't actually spending our time treating addiction. In taking on this business, we were totally responsible for funding, hiring/firing, the daily operational management, all of it.

But as long as we had our passion, we could call upon that to give us energy, and to encourage others to get involved, offer their support, or lend us their talents. As Xavier Helgesen says, "You have to be able to inspire people about the indefinite and uncertain. If [social entrepreneurs] get people fired up about something that doesn't exist yet, they can inspire people like investors and partners to get behind it. It's the creative tension between details and inspiring people to believe it will work" that characterizes the social entrepreneur.

So we set about ironing out the details. We had closed on the building in Salt Lake City, and now were owners of a physical space that would become the beginning foundation our dream. The weight of our responsibility—not just in paying back Arvis's loan and the mortgage on the property, but the responsibility to our employees as well as to those future guests and their family members we would treat—grew heavier each day.

As part of the terms of our arrangement with Arvis, his $1.5 million was loaned to us at an interest rate of 8.25 percent. For the first 12 months, our payments were interest only ($10,000 per month), and that would balloon up to interest plus principal after one year's time, which could increase the payments to $14,000 per month. Our goal was to pay him off in twelve months.

With the $225,000 we had set aside in equity, we began paying him each month with his own money, and would do so until we could generate cash flow through the business. We would then refinance the property, and pay Arvis back in full. In my nightclub experience, I knew about the essential rule to "always pay the house" first.

This meant the clock was ticking; with a $10,000 interest payment to make each month, every day our business wasn't open, we lost more than $300.

So we set daily and weekly goals, milestones we must reach in order to progress along the path to opening our doors to guests. Our first and most important of these goals were:

1. Obtaining a business license, and

2. Hiring the required professionals to oversee the various aspects of the business.

Meanwhile, I spent most of my time setting up the physical location, marketing, branding and traveling back and forth between Las Vegas and Salt Lake City.

In addition to all of this, our daughter, Haley, was born. Lisa spent Haley's first three months home with the baby full time which actually allowed her more time to work on the business, since she wasn't also pulling 12-hour shifts, and while I did what I could to help out at home, I was on the road so often traveling between home and Salt Lake that neither Lisa nor I got much sleep. It crossed our minds frequently that all of this had been a terrible idea.

After three months had passed, Lisa returned to work at the police department, which was essential in maintaining our living expenses. Haley stayed with my mother during Lisa's 12-hour shifts, and I focused all my time and energy on building the business in Salt Lake.

I had a tremendous sense that I was failing—as a new entrepreneur, as a husband, and as a new father. Almost daily I considered running home and throwing in the towel. But the pressure of paying Arvis back, and the deep, intuitive knowledge that this was what I was supposed to be doing—my "why"—kept me at it. The words "there's more work to do" echoed in my mind over and over, and were the often the only things that propelled me.

Fortunately, we both felt so strongly about our "why," because our bad experience with hiring employees and the many obstacles we faced would have caused us to give up otherwise.

To meet our two primary goals, we hired our first official team members. First was Charles, a former associate from the nightclub business whose expertise was sales and marketing, for the Director of Marketing position. It made sense to us that this position should be filled first—if we didn't start attracting guests, we wouldn't have a business.

The other, Richard, a fellow practitioner of martial arts that I'd met in Las Vegas, told me that he had run child and adolescent treatment facilities in Utah and was currently working in the field. He was looking for an employment change and wanted to come on board. With his valuable experience in the licensing process, and his comments that he was "friends with the licensing guys" and knew how to get us a license at the Department of Human Services' Office of Licensing, he seemed a natural fit for our Program Manager position.

For the first month or two, it seemed reasonable that we still had no license. But by the third and fourth months, without a thing to show for it and having by now paid Arvis back $40,000, Lisa and I decided it was time for me to go out to Salt Lake and see for myself what was really going on. Though I'd been traveling there extensively, my time had been filled

Starting a business takes a tremendous amount of time, energy and dedication. While having a newborn, working 12 hour shifts, plus working on the business times full time, throwing in the towel may have seemed like a easy way out. But to have the freedom we wanted and to be a part of the solution, I knew we had to keep going. There would be light at the end of the tunnel eventually. Continuing to stay positive and encouraged was key in the beginning. Having each other as a sounding board and not letting the other get discouraged was a big part of us being a team.

with preparing the 15,000-square-foot building, looking for counselors to work with us, and a myriad of other things that cropped up in my limited time there. Richard had repeatedly told me, "Everything's fine with licensing, don't worry, I'm handling it and we should have it in no time," and I had been more than willing to hand off that task to an "expert," as Charles, Lisa, and I already had so many other items we were working on. But that one bad decision had cost us tens of thousands of precious dollars, and had almost destroyed the business before it even got off the ground.

And we had no guests, either. Until we had a license, we could not admit guests into the program. Charles had been in Las Vegas, waiting for a cue that it was time to move to Utah, and it was time. The two of us moved out there and decided to take matters into our hands. For things to change, first we had to change. And that's exactly what we did.

Charles and I both relocated permanently to Salt Lake City, while Lisa stayed behind in Vegas with Haley, working and supporting the business from there. Every couple of weeks, Lisa would fly up to Utah for a weekend to assist us on site, and so all three of us could collaborate in person instead of by phone.

The first thing I did was meet with Richard's "friends," the licensing authorities at the city and state levels. What I discovered boiled my blood: Not only had Richard angered the licensing board, who were, in fact, *not* his friends, but the so-called expert had been lying to me. We faced a compliance challenge, in that the federal government considers addiction a disability, and views addicts as vulnerable adults. In Utah, the State Department of Human Services also has strict requirements when it comes to obtaining a license. In fact, the qualifications are no different than licensing a special needs home for adults with Down Syndrome or mental illnesses. We had known this going into the licensing request, and Spencer had actually warned us of this. But Richard's lack of know-how and follow-through had actually driven us *further away* from obtaining our licenses in four months, rather than closer. This was much bigger than anything I had expected, and we had a lot of ground to make up.

Throughout the process of developing Journey Healing Centers, we had gotten the sense that the right people kept entering our lives at the right times. Apparently, we, as students, were ready to learn more and more, and the teachers continued to appear. But what we were now realizing was that everywhere we turned, we were encountering valuable lessons, and not all of them were enjoyable. Many lessons, like this one, were downright painful. It was saddening to discover that "friends" were really not friends, or even good employees for that matter. (This is also an important lesson in terms of forming your social enterprise team, but we'll talk more about that later.)

When hiring "friends" make sure they go through your normal hiring processes. Making sure they are a fit for the position and have the skill set is key. It can be painful to not only lose a friendship but to have it hurt the business as well.

Once I got past the initial shock that all the work we had been doing had been insufficient for our license, I made an appointment with the board, and got their list of requirements for achieving licensure. Although we'd had a basic licensing list initially, we discovered that we had not been aware of all the specific details that comprised the core requirements. I felt good to be moving in a positive direction, but it was now clear to me that it would take quite a while to form a positive relationship with them.

Not only that, but aside from the opportunity cost and lost income we were reeling from, we had now lost a combined total of more than $60,000—that was $40K in payments to Arvis, and another $20K+ in operating expenses. It was an expensive lesson, but it's a good thing we learned it at that moment: If we wanted to build our business right and prevent ourselves from being manipulated, we needed to get control of it, and learn all the aspects of the industry that were essential to long-term success. And while we didn't want to become specialists, it served us well to know all aspects in a general sense, so that we knew what questions to ask, whom to ask, and what had to be done to move forward.

I went back to our new office at the Journey location, fully intent on handling licensing myself from then on. It meant a complete overhaul of policies and procedures, which wasn't a strength of mine. Fortunately, with significant input and focus from Lisa and Charles, not to mention many late nights, the three of us pulled together countless forms and compliance documents that were required for licensure.

I took the licensing on myself, and many other things, too—marketing, cleaning floors, cooking, driving, dealing with labor boards (the result of officially letting our Program Manager go), answering phones, working with insurance companies... If we were going to be business owners, it was our job to understand every facet of it. We were really apprenticing in our own business. Lisa and I became generalists in every aspect of the business. We were learning a little about a lot of things. And we vowed to never again trust our livelihood and family's future to someone who says "I know a guy... trust me." There is a big difference between trusting someone when you also know what the job entails, and trusting someone when you don't know.

We got our license to open the first Journey Healing Center in January 2003, and then got to meet our next teacher... a thing called marketing.

Because with all the struggles we'd encountered with licensing, worrying that we wouldn't even have a place to put any guests, we had put our marketing efforts on the back burner. Besides, our research told us that addiction was reaching epidemic levels and demand for private rehabilitation facilities was extremely high. It made sense to us that by simply opening the doors, we'd have clients lining up.

That simply wasn't the case.

Prior to securing our license in January 2003 we felt a sense of desperation to fill rooms and start making an income. The problem was that we still had no refined treatment program and no business license yet in place—a grievous error on our part—and still no good counselors to treat guests. All we wanted at this point was to fill beds with *anyone*, cut any deal we could to bring in some money. We thought about the different ways we could bring in income without a license from the State. We decided to set up a website and begin marketing the property as Sober

Living, a safe and sober living environment for recovering addicts that provided room and board only, not treatment.

A few weeks later, the phone rang from our first official Sober Living customer: Carol from Wyoming. She paid $3,000 per month to live in our facility. Lisa cooked her meals (when she was in town from Vegas), and I cleaned her room and the bathrooms, on top of everything else. We all did what we could to be a safety net for her, talking with her about all the issues that come up in recovery and driving her to AA meetings. It was a lot of work, but it was extraordinarily gratifying to finally be helping someone in a hands-on way, just as we'd dreamed of doing. We were sure to shower her with support and encouragement, and made her feel like family.

We'd have done anything, *anything,* legally, ethically, and morally, to get some revenue, because we were dying. We didn't even have a credit card machine at the time, and had to run Carol's charges through my dad's nightclub business. How's that for irony?

It hit home for us that until we had a license and steady income, we couldn't pay doctors, or therapists, as that would have drained our working capital in just a few months. But how could we get income from clients without hiring on a full staff? It seemed a cruel catch-22.

But through our studies of *Rich Dad*, in particular the *Cashflow Quadrant,* we realized that these professionals were highly educated, highly specialized people who often liked to do things themselves; they like to be paid high hourly rates, on a self-employed ("S") basis, and are less eager to work for a salary. That was perfect for us.

Slowly, very slowly, we found a few contracted doctors, counselors, and therapists who agreed to come on board on an as-needed basis, with payment only for services performed. This structure worked for everyone as a win/win, and we still use it today.

After obtaining our license in January, we began cutting any deal we could just to get people into the system. The original base price we had set for treatment had been $12,000 per month; we were taking some admissions for as little as $1,200, giving it away just to get this as-yet-untested plan off the ground. We knew the program we wanted to build; we had our vision, but we didn't have the full staffing, experience, or capacity yet to do it. As guests began working their way through it, we tested and refined it daily, sometimes hourly, building a supreme program and incorporating our vision.

We spent many a night, agonizing over what would become of our fledgling business, this dream that seemed to encounter obstacle after obstacle, which now also included ongoing attacks from an upset and recently fired Richard (as well as the labor board with whom he had filed a complaint) and the reserves that were drying up fast. How could it be that all the work we'd done, all the pain and heartache we'd experienced, would come to nothing because of money? Why were we being tested at every turn? We really felt as if we'd hit the wall. Perhaps, this time, we really would have to give up.

As typically happens in such a state of emergency, something wonderful emerges. We remembered the Law of Reciprocity: What you give out to the world comes back to you. We had a valuable service that we wanted the world to have access to. Why not follow Robert Kiyosaki's 2nd principle, "Work for free"? Why not serve first and give our service away for free to those who needed it? As bizarre as this may have sounded at the time, this was true to our mission, personally and professionally. We were all about healing with dignity and respect. If that was our "why," then shouldn't that be our first commitment in building our clientele?

We started a 24-hour call-in helpline for anyone wanting information about drugs, alcohol, and addiction. It was enormously satisfying to share what we knew and help others, and we believed, deep down to our cores, that the more we gave of ourselves, the more the universe would provide. Our goal was and continues to be, to provide this service, whether the callers were looking for treatment or not.

At first, Lisa and I divided the helpline between us, splitting it into two 12-hour shifts. After a few months, the calls, which had started out coming once every other day or so, came more and more frequently, until we found ourselves awakened from sound sleep to coach someone through a crisis. As difficult as it was, the pain in their voices, the horrors of their stories gave us more reassurance that what we were doing was the right thing. We had more incentive to keep at it. Moms and dads, sisters and brothers, husbands and wives told us about the misery of losing their loved ones to addiction, how they just wanted their loved ones back. They seemed to take enormous comfort in our ability to connect to their stories, share insights, provide solutions, and reveal how we'd come out the other side.

We knew that, despite the rough patch we were in, there was a great demand for Journey Healing Centers throughout the world, and that it could be tremendously powerful for people. The idea of giving people back their lost loved ones was a simple philosophy that still remains our core promise today.

The helpline was extremely valuable, and the calls weren't the kind we could ever cut off because we had to work in the morning, were tired or were in the middle of dinner. Many a time, we were out at dinner when the calls came, and one of us would end up eating alone as the other stepped outside to talk to someone in crisis. We listened, sometimes for hours, building relationships and becoming entwined in agonizing stories of missing relatives, jail time, deaths, abandoned babies, lost jobs or businesses, and ER visits.

Eventually, the helpline took so much time that we were now in a place to hire more people to answer the growing number of calls for information that the marketing department was producing for us. The call center began to take on a life of its own; we were now in the game, walking in the fields.

We never thought of the helpline as a sales tool, and had no intention of doing so. Unless someone was actively seeking treatment, which they began doing after several months, we served freely, and sought only to assist them through difficult times. It took a little time, but we began growing our clientele and the cash began flowing in.

And when our guests began breaking down in our arms, crying and thanking us for saving their lives and changing them for the better, we absolutely knew that we were on the right path. No amount of money could have been a greater reward to us.

By our ninth month, we had enough cash flow that were no longer paying Arvis back with his own money. And by the end of our first reporting year, by applying the Law of Reciprocity, Journey Healing

Centers was profitable. Lisa was, at this point, able to quit the police department and focus full time on the business, too.

Bottom line: Our "why" got us through all that difficulty, and it was where our eventual success came from. Without constant dedication and commitment to our vision—treating people who struggle with addiction with dignity and respect, supporting them to become free from addiction—do you think we would have stayed with it? Probably not. Heck, I *know* not. Between our lack of initial capital, the effort involved in licensing compliance, employee challenges, angry guests, and our many struggles in getting the business off the ground, we had about a zillion opportunities to quit, and for many people it certainly would have been understandable to do so. For a lot of people in my position, it would have actually been a good excuse to say "screw it" and go get drunk.

A lot of entrepreneurs get an idea, secure a location, get excited about selling the idea to others, and then they run into the endless challenges that eventually cause them to just fold up and go home. They realize they're in over their heads.

That's what we would have done but for one thing: our "why." We got through it and learned a lot in the process, and that made us stronger.

So if we're going to give you any advice about becoming a Social Capitalist, here it is: Find your why, dedicate everything to it, and trust the process. In the end, your "why" is the most important thing you'll have, and it will change your life forever.

We had at this point effectively reached one of our major goals; both of us were no longer employees. We were on our way to building a B business. Having many goals set in place and acknowledging when they are achieved, or as Rich Dad Advisor Blair Singer would say, "celebrate the wins", anchors in the successes and makes the obstacles not seem so heavy.

How to Find Your "Why"

While the best piece of advice we can give you is to find and know your why, it's also the hardest to give, because there's nothing we can say that shows you what your why is. Only you can determine that. It's an incredibly personal thing.

Here are a few questions that can support you in finding your why:

1. What do you like doing?

2. What are you passionate about—is it a cause, or one that's connected to it?

3. Are you, or is someone you know, affected by or involved with this cause?

4. What makes you upset, or connects to your spirit?

5. What is something (or someone) you could not life without?

6. What project do you do and that causes you to lose track of time?

7. What gives you energy?

8. If you could change one thing in this world, what would it be and why?

Michael Holthouse has interviewed and hired thousands of people, and one of the first questions he asks every one of them is this: "What do you do for fun?"

"One, if you tell me what you do for fun, you're telling me what you're good at," Holthouse explains. "If I just sat down and said, 'Tell me, what are you good at?' they start fumbling. But if I'm hiring a salesperson, and he tells me how he spends the weekend curled up with a book at home, that probably tells me I'm not talking to a serious salesperson, who should thrive on being around people. So, by understanding what people love to do, you know their passion and what they're good at ... If you want to create a product or service to excel at, it's got to be fun and a passion, where you get real benefit economically and feel really good about what you stand for, and you thrive off of it."

Something else that's really important to keep in mind is that Social Capitalists often work in their own back yards. Tanyella Evans, "Strategist for Social Entrepreneurs," wrote in an April 2012 article entitled "Heroic vs. Homegrown Entrepreneurs?" for *The Huffington Post*, "When we think of 'social entrepreneurship,' we tend to focus on the really big organizations that have had a huge impact, groups like Teach for America or Grameen that are dealing with national or global issues of poverty, inequality and justice ... Yet research suggests that social entrepreneurship is also making an impact on the local economy."

Evans goes on to point out that groups focused at the community level are equally deserving of our focus, and in a lot of cases, can make a greater impact much more quickly.

In other words, what issues touch you on a daily basis, urging you to act? What idea do you have that would fix a problem in your own back yard? Because that, right there, is your why.

For us, this was the lifesaving power of addiction recovery. For Kreece Fuchs and Xavier Helgesen, it was a wasted pile of books in the apartment and a community center that needed some books. For Muhammad Yunus, it was the hungry people outside his classroom window.

What's yours?

Another great question is to ask them where they see themselves in five years, or what would they like to be doing in five years. Many in an interview setting will make it goal oriented towards the job they are doing but if you can get them to open up about their passion, you will see if it relates to the position they are applying for. And while we are always wanting employees for life, we also know that by letting someone tap into their passion, they may be one of the best employees/contractors while they are with you. Or their passion may keep them with you long term but knowing where they want to be and acknowledging that empowers them to be the best they can be.

Chapter Thought

If your motivation to work is money, you are a slave to money. If you're working to achieve a mission, you are free. Money is just a by-product of doing something you love and feel connected to.

Chapter Six

The Fight

"Your time is limited, so don't waste it living someone else's life. Don't be trapped by dogma — which is living with the results of other people's thinking. Don't let the noise of others' opinions drown out your own inner voice. And most important, have the courage to follow your heart and intuition. They somehow already know what you truly want to become. Everything else is secondary."

—Steve Jobs, Stanford University Commencement
Address, June 12, 2005

In 1976, when Julie Smolyansky was just one year old, her family emigrated from the former Soviet Union and settled in Chicago, Illinois. Julie's father found work as a mechanical engineer, and her mother began working as a manicurist. Two years later, the Smolyansky family opened a Russian delicatessen offering Eastern European foods for the area's Russian population.

Julie's mother, who had come to the U.S. with an infant daughter at just 26, without knowing a word of English, helped unload trucks and manage the family's finances to assist with building the deli into a dominant Russian food business in Illinois. Meanwhile, Julie's father often spent his limited free time counseling new immigrants on assimilating into American culture and our ways of doing business. He often advised them on starting businesses here, helping them, in turn, to make their own businesses successful.

"It's just how I was brought up," Julie says, who inherited business acumen and a sense of compassion and responsibility for helping others from her parents. "It was just that way in our family—'help people when you can, always.'"

When the family made a food-buying trip to Germany in 1985, they got their first taste of kefir, a fermented milk drink that was a staple in the Soviet Union. They returned to the U.S. and began Lifeway Foods, which is now the country's leading manufacturer of kefir. The company went public in 1988. And when Julie's father passed unexpectedly in 2002, leaving Julie as the unwitting CEO at just 27, it made her the youngest female CEO of a publicly traded company.

She's passionate about the work Lifeway does, producing a natural, organic product that has been shown to have medicinal properties and aid in preventing certain conditions such as Crohn's Disease and irritable bowel syndrome. But as the daughter of a strong, independent woman, as well as the CEO of a large corporation and the mother of two daughters, Julie's also passionate about the empowerment and support of women everywhere.

Times have certainly changed from when our grandparents and many of our parents grew up. Women are becoming more empowered to run and lead successful businesses and move away from the stereotypical "women's place is in the home" mentality. And while homemaking is a very worthy profession, it's great many women are also a part of opportunities and involved in investments and finances with spouses. There are many women paving the road for others to be leaders and take control of who they are and who they want to be.

"Women occupy 52 percent of the population but only 18 hold the CEO positions in *Fortune 500* companies, and only 17 percent of women hold seats in Congress," she says. "I want to make sure my daughters' world is better than ours."

This hit home for her when she visited Bangladesh in summer of 2011 as part of Every Mother Counts, Christy Turlington Burns' advocacy and mobilization campaign for global maternal health. Having visited urban slums and acid violence centers, and learning that Bengali men are actually allowed to throw acid on women that reject them or whom they believe are committing adultery, she became a passionate fighter in the cause of giving women a hand up out of poverty and violence.

With Julie spearheading, Lifeway has lent its voice to Every Mother Counts through marketing, advocacy, awareness campaigns, fundraising events, and leadership, in addition to charitable donations.

"I believe that every single moment in my past has brought me to where I am today," Julie says. "As a matter of fact, I think much of my past, including the most difficult of times, has fueled my passions, drive, work ethic, and fighter spirit. It has also helped create a forever positive, optimistic spirit and personal ideology that 'this too shall pass' on my hardest of days."

That "fighter spirit" can only come from one's own fight. As Julie said, "every single moment in my past has brought me to where I am today." Take a moment and reflect upon your past. What is fueling your passion and drive? What's *your* fight?

Our Fight

They say "pick your battles," and it's an important lesson. Any kind of entrepreneurship is hard; it's only worth fighting to stay alive if the fight is personal, and the business is something that truly represents what you stand for. Because you'll always have people telling you that you can't do it, and you're going to have to fight your way past them. Make sure it's worth it.

For Julie Smolyansky, fighting for girls and women makes good sense. "I personally believe that the beginning of my life, from age 0 to 35, was for me," she says, "and that the rest of my life is dedicated to my children and the world."

For us, obviously, the fight against addiction is personal and dear to us. It wouldn't make sense for us to open an animal rescue center or improve irrigation systems in third-world countries. Although very important, we are not driven to invest the countless amount of time, energy, and passion that would be required to launch those enterprises. Hearing about a problem, following your family's passion, or being moved by it doesn't mean it's the best foundation upon which to build your own social enterprise. Our point here is that it must be personal for you, something tied to your heart, your memories, your passion, and your history. Fight *your* fight, not somebody else's.

Chapter Thought

To identify your fight, ask yourself the following: What makes you mad? What gets under your skin so much that there's no end to the energy you can find to fight it? Is there something you're passionate about, something so personal that you feel you must do something about it? Maybe it *is* clean water in Africa, even if you've never been there, but it should strike your heart so dearly that it is a must in your life.

As we got Journey Healing Centers off the ground, our ongoing research showed that the problem was not just alcohol or illegal drugs. The world has experienced a massive boom in prescription drug use. Millions of people are prescribed medications by well-intentioned but lawsuit-averse physicians who have little to no training in addiction. Pain management drugs, which are administered in hospital settings, are often sent home with patients who can, and often do, become addicted. Add the fact that an estimated 800,000 websites now make it easy to purchase prescription drugs online, without a doctor's approval. As the pharmaceutical companies evolve, there are increasing numbers of stronger pain pills coming on the market, so the risk of becoming addicted and experiencing serious physical withdrawals, or even death, is greater than ever.

Just take a look in your home's medicine cabinet, and really look carefully at the medications in there. I think you'll be surprised by what you find.

Of even more concern is the fact that young people are having "pharm parties," raiding their parents' and friends' medicine cabinets and throwing what they find into bowls for a sick kind of drug roulette, everyone popping pills and chasing them with alcohol. Many times they even roll dice to see how many pills to take on their turns. According to the National Institute on Drug Abuse, in a 2010 survey, an estimated 20 percent of Americans had used prescription drugs for nonmedical uses, and more than half of them were ages 12-17.

It's sickening that the media's portrayal of drinking and partying is only concerned with the fun, but it rarely shows what happens later, when the fun stops and the pain begins. Sure, it's okay to party, but it's not okay to have a problem, and many times people don't know they've crossed that line until it's too late.

Then there are the misleading ads about prescription drugs, with their miniscule attempts to educate people about the potential for abuse and addiction.

As you can see, we could go on and on. We guarantee that you and you children will be exposed to drugs and alcohol in your lives. As parents, knowing this feels like fire in our bellies. We know our fight is an uphill battle, but we have absolutely no intention of quitting. You know why? Because we lived with addiction, and have personally experienced its destructive power. Addiction nearly destroyed our lives and has taken the lives of so many of our friends. We will *never* stop fighting it, personally and professionally.

That's not to say that sometimes we didn't feel like stopping. While still in the planning, and even after we opened our doors, we went through a tremendous number of ups and downs. One minute we felt like we were geniuses, and the next minute we felt like we were idiots. The emotional roller coaster gave us a real case of the "screw-its." Things got tough and I'd say "Screw it, I'm done." Fortunately, I had a solid support system behind me, and the realization that by quitting, I was putting more than my sobriety at risk. I was also risking my wife, my child, my business, our investor, and my employees. The two of us had way too much at stake to stop fighting. I had built the perfect environment to support my sobriety.

Now my sobriety was bigger than me. I had much more on the line, and it was not worth throwing away for a drunken stupor. So addiction was both our nemesis and our driving force.

Being committed to letting the world know that those that struggle from addiction are not "bad" people, they just made mistakes and got caught up in something they couldn't control and deserved assistance in finding their way back is part of our fight.

And it gave us an unfair advantage over other treatment centers and their leadership. These guests, they were *my* people, my tribe. I knew what they were up against, and I saw better ways to deliver healing programs than what was out there at the time. I knew that overcoming addiction could happen with dignity and respect. All my life's experiences seemed to culminate in building Journey Healing Centers, and every step along my own journey and Lisa's had led us here. This was our purpose, or some could even call it our destiny.

However, that didn't carry much weight when Charles and I hit the street for our "road show," our name for our ongoing effort to interest counselors in joining our treatment team and support a referral relationship. We knocked on a lot of doors, shook a lot of hands, distributed a lot of brochures, and performed our "spiel" for a lot of professionals in behavioral health. And, surprisingly, we got a lot of doors slammed in our faces. The ones that actually heard us out were incensed by our slick performance and arrogance over believing we had any right, as uneducated nightclub workers, to run a legitimate treatment center, and they promptly suggested that we go back to school and get degrees in counseling, like they had done. Then they politely asked us to leave.

Concerned about our inability to build a network of customer referrals, which we believed would be our bread and butter, we hired a University of Utah professor to consult with us on building our business. After taking a few notes about our struggle, she agreed with the counselors. "You don't know what you're doing," she argued. "You really need to go back to school." She then billed us $750 for these insights, and considered her job complete and her recommendations helpful.

It was devastating to hear that none of the professionals we wanted to build relationships with would support us. What was the most upsetting was that Charles and I knew there were countless numbers of people struggling with and dying from addiction. How dare these professionals deny referrals to a center that could possibly save a life? Because we were not in what we saw as their Ivy League clique, with long acronyms after our names, we were outsiders.

Were we not fighting the same fight?

The mistake we made by hiring the professor to consult us on the business, was that she had never been in business herself, at least not at the time. She may have been a great teacher but she was not an entrepreneur and we realized were not speaking the same language. She only taught the ideas and theories in school. Her training told her to go to school, get good grades and *then* attempt business. This was not our path.

Yet, there were two things we knew that none of these professionals did:

1. We were business owners, not self-employed counseling professionals. We were not building jobs, like they did, we were building a business. To use *Rich Dad* terminology, we were B people talking to S people. We had no intention of treating our guests ourselves, but only of creating a space in which such work could happen. For that, we were trained to think like business people, not self-employed counselors. They were the experts in the counseling field, and we wanted them on our team doing what they did best, so that we could do what we did best and run the business.

2. Their degrees and years of professional experience didn't tell them a lot of what I had lived through. I'd been there and done that when it came to addiction. I started testing my theory and would ask them, "Are you a friend of Bill W.?" Invoking the name

of the founder of Alcoholics Anonymous was often a code for those of us in the world of alcoholism recovery, and anyone with real experience in the field would know that. But, shockingly, many of the addiction counselors we spoke with didn't. How could they talk to anyone effectively about overcoming drug and alcohol addiction if they'd never experienced it or been affected by it personally? Experience goes a lot further than learning about it in school.

Understanding these two important points convinced us that it was important to stop talking to the smart yet inexperienced academics and counselors with lots of letters behind their names, and start talking to people working on the ground, in the field of addiction, every day. Those people were passion-driven, school *and* street educated. In other words, those people had a strong "why." That simple approach changed everything. We began recruiting others who were fighting the same fight. Because it felt personal to them, too, they had a stake in an innovative solution like ours. They had both the schooling necessary to conduct therapy and the "street smarts" from having either been there themselves or having gone through it with loved ones of their own.

It's important when networking and building relationships to find those that have the same why or passion. While relationships will also be built with many who have different passions, you will find the biggest supporters have a personal why to be connected to what you do.

As hard as it was to have knowledgeable professionals whom we respected at the time tell us what we were doing was wrong—validating every insecurity I'd ever had as a kid—it was crucial to Journey's success. Had we not taken those beatings and many others, from every person and organization that told us we didn't know what we were doing and we should quit immediately, we would not be as strong as we are today.

This one bit of knowledge, this understanding of our brand advantage, came from getting knocked down and not being willing to stay down. It came from using our solid "why" to drive everything we do. The fight came to us, and we met it head-on.

It's not the hardship that matters, it's what you do with it. With ours, Lisa and I could very easily have beaten ourselves up. But we turned our dark times into light, and we, and our business, grew stronger. With every struggle, we found ourselves in an increasingly better position to serve. It's through that and our unfair advantage that we became, and continue to be, successful.

Fighting Words

In a study about the mindset of children toward people with disabilities, Harvard psychologist Ellen Langer visited a school and presented children in several classrooms with a picture of someone in a wheelchair. She asked the children, "Can this person drive a car?"

Overwhelmingly, as you can imagine, their answer was "no."

Then, she visited different classrooms, and in these, she changed the question to, "How can this person drive a car?"

Well, as children typically do, they were able to provide Langer with a multitude of creative answers to that question.

Guclu, Dees, and Anderson share this example in their article for CASE entitled "The Process of Social Entrepreneurship" to illustrate a very important characteristic of the social entrepreneur: "Successful social entrepreneurs embody this 'how can' attitude," they write, "particularly in the idea generation phase. How can I translate my personal experience into broad social impact?"

Even with Lisa's preparation with the police department and mine running nightclubs (both of us frequently dealing with potentially violent and dangerous people), we were constantly being faced with unexpected situations in owning our business that threw us for a loop. But as the business continued to grow, and we finally found and continued to refine a committed team and a growing clientele base, we also had to grow and evolve with it, sometimes in ways that felt foreign to us.

But looking back, we're glad that we had jobs that forced us to face and conquer many of our fears with every shift, because it turned us into people who don't say "We can't," but who say, "How *can* we?"

Robert Kiyosaki's book *Choose To Be Rich* wasn't just a good title; it became a sort of mantra for us. It implied that we'd made a choice. We didn't just *want* a different life, or *desire* wealth. We chose it. It's an incredibly empowering idea. That one little distinction, that one-word difference portrays a canyon-sized chasm between wishing for something and making it happen. We chose this life; we made a declaration, took control, and commanded the universe to provide that for us. Choice became our way of life. And that word had a trickle-down effect in all aspects of our lives. We choose the words we use, the thoughts we have, and the actions we take.

We realized that once we chose to be rich, not only did it set us on a course of continual lifelong learning; it affected *every* other choice we made. From where we worked to how we spent our time, to the people we associated with, to our unwillingness to let failure of any sort stop us, we had made a choice and we weren't going back on it. To us, putting our choice into action, making the tough decisions, doing the difficult things was what it meant to *choose* to be rich, in health, wealth, and happiness.

Actions were a big part of transforming our lives, but so was language. We began to look at the words we were using. The words we use can empower us, or take power from us. Almost every day, we would ask ourselves, "Is this a word of increase or a word of decrease? Is this word assisting us in our goals or is it getting in the way of our progress?"

We discovered some words could take over our vocabulary and covertly undermine us. We call them "parasite words." We all have them and they are words we use thoughtlessly, without purpose, over and over again, as they unintentionally betray our doubt and fear to the world.

How many of these words and phrases do you use each day?

Kind of (or "kinda," as in "I kinda work out.") How do you "kinda" anything? You either work out or you don't. "Kind of," or "kinda," expresses nothing more than a lack of commitment. You're in between, on the fence. It can demonstrate a weak constitution.

I'm trying (as in, "I'm trying to stay sober.") Think about it—there's really no such thing as *trying* to do something. When we hear people say that, it tells us there is a back door, and it likely won't happen. If someone invites you to lunch and you say, "I'll try to come," it's pretty much a given that you won't make it, you just don't have the strength to stand in your power and say no.

I'm thinking (as in, "I'm thinking about starting a business." Or "I think so.") Again, when we hear this phrase, any meaningful action is unlikely. It implies a lack of knowledge or certainty. It's a word of inaction and procrastination.

Need (as in, "You need to get a job.") We heard this a lot when we were starting Journey Healing Centers: "You need to go back to school," or "You need to be a counselor." Is there anything that implies more lack? We consider this word to be energy-draining; its mere existence in a sentence implies lack, dependence, failure. Neediness is desperate. The word holds poor intentions, rests in inactivity, and takes rather than gives. Better word choices would be "choose," "deserve," and "get to."

Help (as in, "Help me!") This word conveys desperation and a lack of personal power, which isn't at all empowering. Instead, we use the words "assistance" or "assist." This enables you to keep your power rather than give it away.

Cheap (as in "Buy this one, it's cheaper.") This word has connotations of value that are separate from price. That makes us feel like we're settling for poor quality. Instead, we want "inexpensive."

Should (as in, "You should go back to school and get a degree.")
People with no authority and no experience often act as though they know what's best for others. We weren't going to fall into the trap of "should-ing all over people."

Words have tremendous power and energy. They can even have an impact on our physical health. Test it out for yourself.

One day, as Lisa was getting a few things done for the business, she told me, "I'm tired."

You say that a lot," I commented, because she did. We were both tired—exhausted, even—but Lisa had been saying it a lot, and it was almost as if that word *made* her more tired. She realized that indeed she had been saying it a lot, and for no reason. After all, why do we feel compelled to announce to people how tired we are? What good does that do? Are we just looking for someone who will sympathize with us? Does it relieve our tiredness? Of course not.

There may be times these words do work but start looking at how often you use them and be open to changing your context of these words and see what a difference they make in how you feel.

She chose then and there to stop saying those two words, or at least to stop announcing her fatigue to the world. Interestingly enough, her seemingly unending exhaustion began to evaporate. She stopped declaring it to the world, and the tiredness began to lose its power.

As a migraine sufferer for most of her life, Lisa also made the decision to no longer announce aloud, or even to herself, when she had a headache. Before long, she started to notice that her headaches were getting further and further apart until she now rarely has them. Words matter.

For myself, after my own rehab, addiction was still a part of our lives. It was always on the periphery, an opponent I fought each day, and so far I had been winning the battle for my own mind and body.

I'd often heard "Hello, my name is _____ and I'm a alcoholic." I would be attending an Alcoholics Anonymous meeting and listening to a person with 20 years of sobriety declaring to the world that he was still an alcoholic.

"I am" is one of the most powerful statements we can use; it's a statement of complete presence, of having a physical experience. It always seemed to me that by constantly living in that experience from 20 years prior, that person is keeping him or herself from moving forward and evolving, moving past the problem.

This idea contradicts the pervasive beliefs of the recovery community (we have a lot more thoughts on this), but,

> *There is another saying, this one from the Bible: "Physician, heal thyself." This has proven true in many instances in our lives. We look at the words we use around the ailment and choose to be healthy. In our experience, miracles do happen.*

as they say, the words are made flesh. It is our truth, that ones body maybe alcoholic, but ones spirit, the I am... is not.

Words have the power to heal and the power to hurt. And when you choose, intentionally *choose*, the words of increase, they will shape your beliefs and your future. When Lisa and I started to change our language, our thinking began to change. It was an important step in changing our lives.

Successful Social Capitalists don't approach a fight asking, "I can't win this fight. Can I really feed the hungry, assist the poor, or solve this problem?" Instead, they ask, "*How* can we solve it? What steps do we take? What don't we know yet?" They never stop asking those questions until they've found a satisfactory answer, the one that will end the fight.

So here are our tips for identifying, and successfully fighting, your fight:

1. Take at least ten minutes and write down what makes you upset. Then ask yourself, "Why?" If you ask that enough times, you will discover your core fight.

2. Look at the words you use. Write a list of words you use repeatedly. We all have words that take over our vocabularies, our "go-to"

words. They are called parasite words. Are you addicted to them? Ask yourself, "Are these words giving me energy or taking energy away?" Then choose words that give you power, words that heal and change how you think. You'll be surprised at the benefits this will have on you and those around you!

Choose your fight accordingly, know it and believe in it at your core, and know that you can make a difference!

Chapter Thought

Physically test the words you use on a regular basis. Ask someone to assist you with this experiment: As you say each word, place your arm straight out and have the other person apply pressure against your arm, pushing it downward. If it's a word of increase, your body will be stronger. If it's a word of decrease, your body will be weaker.

Chapter Seven

Global Resources for Social Capitalists

"What investors want is the equivalent of lighting a match in a room where a propane tank has been open for 20 minutes."

-Jon Carson, CEO and Chairman, BiddingforGood.com

We were fortunate that by utilizing *Rich Dad* principles for financial freedom—such as creating something out of nothing (or ephemeralization, as Bucky Fuller called the idea of doing more with less until eventually you can do everything with nothing), using other people's money, and leveraging business opportunities by using the B/I triangle—financing for the first Journey Healing Center, as well as for the five additional centers we eventually added, was a process that was repeated and became relatively easier. We say "relatively," because many entrepreneurs don't make it past the first year and have the opportunity to see that the process just repeats. The only difference, really, is in the number of zeros. After each year, we have reflected on the dumb mistakes we've made and gotten smarter.

Of course, as we've shared with you, it wasn't exactly *easy* for us to find funding to get started. As a matter of fact, that first year and our first attempt to secure capital was the most difficult, because we had nothing to show for our hard work and no track record in the field. But we raised the money, survived the ups and downs, and within one year of being in business, we found ourselves with a profitable company. That's a big deal when you consider that three out of every ten small businesses fail in the first year, according to the Small Business Administration and then ultimately 9 out of 10 fail in ten years.

While that figure may be astounding, having a sound business plan, financial education, emotional intelligence, a strong "why," and persistence all increase those odds.

Neither of us had ever received even a basic financial education. Heck, we didn't even know what a financial education was. Prior to our experience with Journey, we thought we knew what it meant to be "rich," of course; we had believed this meant that you never had to fight over paying the bills, and you could buy anything or go anywhere you wanted. When I asked my parents to buy me something, they often replied with, "Who do you think you are, Rockefeller?" or "Money doesn't grow on trees!" Sound familiar?

We were both taught that in order to have money and become rich, we would have to go to school, get good jobs, save up, and pay off our debts. (Or, even better, we could become a movie star, a professional athlete, a doctor, a lawyer, or a high-level government worker.) There was little to no discussion about how to make money in a way that didn't mean getting a "good" job, or how to create money from nothing, let alone something as mystifying and potentially risky as investing, or using money to make money.

To Lisa's family, savings accounts or a 401K were the only ways to grow money; that *was* investing. To my father, the idea of giving his cash to someone else to hold onto or invest was absurd; he believed banks served one purpose, and that was to enable him to have a checking account, so that he could pay his vendors and his employees. In his line of work (and, for a while, mine, too), cash was king, and it was something to protect at all costs, which is why we carried handguns.

So you can see why neither of us understood money well enough to know how to secure enough of it to start our business. Really, we didn't understand what money was. But thanks to my dad's suggestion of, and connection to, a "private wealthy," along with insights from Robert

Kiyosaki and, later, Arvis, a new financial understanding had begun to dawn on us.

As I've said before, by making mistakes, we got smarter with each passing year. Mistakes are a good thing, as long as you learn from them, and are willing to make them. We're taught in school that it's bad to make mistakes, so we grow up afraid of them; consequently, we don't take chances or seize opportunities.

For instance, one of the services we overlooked was the demand for after-care to complement the services Journey offered, so that clients who had completed their 28 days of rehab could retain ongoing treatment. And we also knew that in order to grow effectively and leverage our business, it was important for us to add locations that served at all levels of care. As we got smarter, we purchased a luxury, six-bedroom/three-bathroom property in Sandy, Utah that would serve those looking for long-term residential treatment at an affordable price; Creekside, as we called it, opened in November 2003. Additionally, we added a four-unit condo property nearby that became our new Sober Living facility, which served as a long-term housing option for those looking for additional life skills, support, and a safe living environment; that opened the following March.

The business was running smoothly and we could have stopped there. But we know that, in order to have a "B" business, according to *Rich Dad*, we had to expand into another state. This would be a true test to see whether our systems would hold—whether we had built a *true* business or a job. In late 2004, we had expanded into Arizona. We opened another treatment center, Sundance Center, in Scottsdale in September 2004, and in September of 2007 we opened The Retreat, an executive-level, long-term care center, also in Scottsdale. The system was working! We now knew that we had a true *Rich Dad* business, and one that was expandable.

Sometimes you don't know what you don't know. As you grow your business, there is always something that will come up that is new to you or you may not have thought of. Be aware of the big picture and the many possibilities out there as you start, grow or expand your business.

For the next few years, we continued to reinvest in our infrastructure, building a better team. And in early 2012, we opened a 6,000-square-foot Journey Healing Centers global headquarters, which also contains an outpatient healing center, in Scottsdale, Arizona. This new platform will allow us to expand, with many more healing centers in the United States, and to launch our international franchise system. Again, using the *Rich Dad* principles of leveraging with licensure and providing commercial opportunities to other like-minded people, our healing centers will now expand throughout the world.

All this growth put pressure on our systems; up until this point, all our facilities had been within blocks of each other, but now we were playing a much bigger game. We had to develop processes, systems, and structures that attracted the best team of professionals to operate the healing centers in multiple locations.

That also meant solidifying our mission and avoiding mission drift, or the tendency to recalibrate or change our mission due to external pressure. When we'd first opened our doors, we would take any and everyone who walked in, and that included employees and contractors, at any price, just to get the job done and the bills paid, and to provide the necessary services. We weren't a mature business, and didn't fully comprehend the value of the work we did. This lesson was invaluable, because we had been giving it away, which in turn caused guests and staff to undervalue the product.

Determine a price for your product or services and stick with it. You can always offer promotions, scholarships and discounts. As the business matures, you may adjust the price based off cost models and valuation of the product or service. Even though we had a price set in the beginning, many times we asked what they could afford rather than start at our price and go from there.

But as we identified the professionals who were attracted to working for us, for the right reasons and in connection to the mission, we realized that many of us didn't relate to the tough-love, court-ordered types of treatment so often associated with addiction. We didn't want to beat up our clients; we wanted to assist them while they stood on their own feet. After all, our clients were really good already at beating themselves up and didn't need us to do that for them. And that's not to say that we don't hold them accountable; when our clients commit to staying sober, we hold them to their word, because we care so much for them that we keep them honest, and the truth is often hard to hear. We create an environment conducive to healing, inside and out.

Success Factors

What's funny is that our street experiences connect closely to the findings of Harvard Business School and Dalberg Global Development Advisors, who conducted a survey of social entrepreneurs. The findings are revealed in a December 2011 report entitled "Learning from Leaders in a Fast-Growing Field," which shows that the three things that were absolutely crucial to our success are the three things that social entrepreneurs cited as most important:

1. A solid team
2. Focus on the social mission (and avoiding mission drift)
3. Financing

Respondents overwhelmingly said that financing was the biggest obstacle to success.

Initial financing was certainly a big challenge to the survey respondents. But for most, securing the larger funding necessary to take a business from the start-up phase to the next level, to become a self-sustaining entity, was the bigger challenge.

Mirjam Schöning says that she's seen this in her experiences with Schwab.

"Many people claim that at the initial stages it's very difficult, but I'd claim that it's healthy," she says. "In a traditional business sense, angel investment isn't easy to find. But you do have several early-stage funds in the U.S., Europe, and the emerging markets. The big gap is when social entrepreneurs come out of the earliest stages, and they need expansion financing. In the range between $200,000, which is too high for foundations, and $2 million, which investors see as too small a ticket, no one finances them. And that's probably the area where most social entrepreneurs are, unfortunately."

"The financing sector is a mess, no doubt about it," remarks Bill Drayton, CEO and founder of Ashoka, which is widely considered to be the first social entrepreneurship-oriented organization. "The citizen sector is still 95 percent stuck in terms of institutional finance having to rely on foundations and government. This gap between the social entrepreneur's garage and having a long-term base of support is a structural problem."

In an article entitled "Funding growth of social businesses," which appears in the Credit Suisse Research Institute's publication *Investing for impact: How social entrepreneurship is redefining the meaning of return*, investment expert Julia Balandina says, "[I]t is extremely hard for social entrepreneurs to access expansion finance, while impact investors are struggling to find mature investable social businesses. The sector needs nurturing growth capital to fund and support social enterprises beyond the start-up phase, enabling them to develop a track record of social value creation and financial sustainability."

Drayton suggests that the two primary sources of this type of funding, foundations and government agencies, are both flawed. Foundations, he says, have no nervous system: "Nothing connects them with their clients. They don't have to listen. They're like the old colonial masters, many meet them at the airport and 'yes massah' them to get what they need, but there's little real respect in those communications."

The government does have a nervous system, Drayton says, and politically it must listen, but it often moves to those who are highly organized and have shared interests —for example, the contractors before the poor family in need.

The truth is, for many investors, it's sexy to fund the hottest new thing. The media tends to focus heavily on the fashionable, while the proven ideas fall by the wayside. Unfortunately, those proven ideas may provide better returns.

Bruce McNamer with TechnoServe says that while there simply isn't enough available capital to infuse into social enterprises, he also believes that a big part of the problem is the inability of the available funds out there to actually connect with the right people.

"There is capital available, but very often it can't find the good small businesses to invest in. Or it can, but that business isn't ready yet to use that capital, or they don't have a plan, or they can't describe how the cash flows. And then businesses say they can't find capital. So a matchmaking process has to happen," McNamer says. "In some cases the money is chasing the same two or three entrepreneurs. So you'll find Funds X, Y, and Z are chasing the same enterprise because they can't find enough of them who are ready to use those funds in the right way."

So what is often the case with social entrepreneurs, even those with groundbreaking ideas, is that they require a host of support measures in order to develop strong, sustainable business plans; identify like-minded mentors and colleagues with whom to do business or consult; locate sources of adequate funding when it's needed; and develop relationships with foundations, other businesses, nonprofits, or the people they intend to serve.

An increasing supply of this support is available, thanks to a new breed of organization designed to sustain the work of social entrepreneurs around the world.

Ashoka: Innovators for the Public

Launched in 1980 in Washington, D.C. by Bill Drayton, a Harvard, Oxford, and Yale educated attorney and former Assistant Administrator for the Environmental Protection Agency, Ashoka was founded on the idea that the most effective way to promote positive social change is to invest in social entrepreneurs with sustainable, big, innovative solutions.

Named after an extraordinarily creative, tolerant, and global-minded Indian leader who renounced violence and dedicated his life to social welfare in the third century B.C., Ashoka works in more than 80 countries around the world, supporting social entrepreneurship in a number of ways:

- Identifying and investing in leading social entrepreneurs (today there are roughly 3,000 of these Ashoka Fellows) in order to help launch and support them in achieving maximum impact

- Promoting group entrepreneurship by enabling hundreds of top social entrepreneurs working on the same problem to think and act together

- Building an infrastructure that supports social entrepreneurs and strengthens the sector, which includes locating or providing seed financing and capital, and facilitating collaborations between sectors (business, academia, government).

The Skoll Foundation

Created by Jeff Skoll in 1999, The Skoll Foundation's mission (according to its website) is to "drive large scale change by investing in, connecting and celebrating social entrepreneurs and the innovators who help them solve the world's most pressing problems."

It does this in a number of ways:

- Supporting education in the field through its partnership with the Said Business School at Oxford University. Begun in 2003, the Skoll Centre for Social Entrepreneurship became the first academic center dedicated to this field. The Skoll Centre provides funding to five MBA students each year who demonstrate a previous track record of, and ongoing commitment to, social innovation, as part of their Skoll Skollars program.

- Providing venture-capital-funded grants through its Skoll Awards for Social Entrepreneurship program

- Making program-related investments through partner financial institutions (banks, equity investment, guarantees)

- Making mission-aligned endowments that enable Skoll to generate income, grow assets over time, and invest in aligned companies or products

- Fostering peer exchange and mentorship through its Skoll World Forum, the premier conference on social entrepreneurship, and SocialEdge.org, its online community of social entrepreneurs.

- Facilitating collaborations between businesses, foundations, nonprofits, and social entrepreneurs (including Ashoka, CASE, and others) that make for effective, long-lasting changes, shape public policy, and advance innovation.

- Spreading the word about the work of social entrepreneurs through a commitment to storytelling through broadcast and film.

An interesting side note: Xavier Helgesen was named a Skoll Skollar for 2010/2011 for his work with Better World Books. It was through that program that he met his partner in his newest venture, Off.Grid:Electric. This distributed renewable energy company in Tanzania began as a research project at Oxford. It capitalizes on the idea that people in developing countries could pay for power, rather than costly renewable energy systems, which would advance the use of renewable energy.

Echoing Green

Founded in 1987 by General Atlantic in an effort to make a greater philanthropic impact, global nonprofit Echoing Green was named for a William Blake poem that speaks of creating a better world.

- Its cornerstone is a fellowship program that has, to date, provided more than 500 Fellows in more than 40 countries with $31 million in start-up funding for their groundbreaking ideas for positive systemic change.

- Additionally, Echoing Green's "ecosystem" is a community of entrepreneurs, conscious capitalists, and investors who collaborate and share ideas and talent through its online forum.

- Its Social Investment Council is a community of leaders and changemakers who are committed to raising funds (their own and others') for Fellows, and to supporting positive global change. They provide insights to and important connections for social entrepreneurs.

- Echoing Green's *Work on Purpose* program challenges Millennials to find work that is both right for them and good for the world. Through the *Work on Purpose* activity and discussion book, workshops, and online community, the largest generation in history can learn how to change their own lives and the world for the better.

Schwab Foundation for Social Entrepreneurship

The Schwab Foundation was established in 2000 by Klaus and Hilde Schwab, who founded the World Economic Forum. In the 1990s, the Schwabs had encountered Muhammad Yunus, who, along with other innovators, inspired them to create a separate foundation to identify innovative bottom-up solutions with an impact on poverty, health education, or other social and environmental challenges. In concert with the World Economic Forum, the Schwab Foundation brings social entrepreneurs to events such as the Forum's Annual Meeting in Davos, where global leaders together at the macro level—including approximately 40 heads of state and prime ministers, CEOs of *Fortune 500* companies, academics, and media leaders—have an opportunity to connect and interact with them and learn first-hand about their models.

Developed to identify leading social entrepreneurs and build the field, the Schwab Foundation provides a number of helpful functions for social entrepreneurs:

- The Foundation holds national Social Entrepreneur of the Year Awards throughout the world, as well as regional competitions in Africa, Latin America, the Middle East, Europe, and Asia. Roughly 1,000 applicants are screened, and the winners are selected to be part of the Foundation's exclusive, valuable global network, and are invited to attend the World Economic Forum's regional and global events, including the Annual Meeting at Davos, Switzerland.

- The Foundation fosters peer-to-peer exchange and collaboration through its global community. "We're an interesting springboard to other regions, so it allows social entrepreneurs to spearhead into new countries and continents," says Foundation Head Mirjam Schöning. "Their innovations find important contacts with government heads or CEOs. That's part of our aspiration; we contribute to spreading those models and innovations, but also to creating ambassadors to build the field, and to providing support and assistance to new social entrepreneurs coming up."

- Though Schwab does not invest financially in any of the social entrepreneurs it works with, it will often cover expenses for travel to World Economic Forum events. And it has created a social investment manual, which is a tool for social entrepreneurs wanting to raise capital from investors. This tool is fairly new, and impact investors are constantly coming online; however, many social entrepreneurs lack the knowledge to access those funds, and many funds aren't very serious, Schöning says. This manual was devised to provide information about the serious funds, as well as their selection criteria, and it also provides information about the kinds of capital that make sense for each entrepreneur, how to know when they're ready to access capital, and what language is useful for jumpstarting that conversation.

- The Schwab Foundation is also developing a governance tool that would guide leaders on how to establish regulations that support social entrepreneurship and leverage capital flows.

Investing for Impact

A new breed of investment capital has emerged in recent years that is intended specifically to support enterprises with social returns. With impact investing, the idea of return on investment is more than monetary; investors no longer only have a choice between investing in start-ups or donating to nonprofits. While of course they seek modest financial returns through investment in social enterprises, they primarily seek social change as their investment goal.

The nonprofit Global Impact Investing Network projects that the impact investment market will grow to $500 billion USD by 2014, which is an average growth rate since 2009 of nearly 60 percent.

Credit Suisse says that investing in companies and projects themselves isn't the only way to invest for impact. Other ways include:

- **Environmental Bonds:** Green bonds and climate bonds are like normal, tradable bonds, except that they are only issued to raise money for environmental projects or climate change mitigation projects. Returns on these bonds are typically tax-exempt.

- **Vaccine Bonds**: According to Credit Suisse, these bonds "convert multi-year foreign aid commitments into immediate cash so vaccines can be administered earlier and to more people."

- **Social Impact Bonds:** These bonds channel funding into social programs, with government paying interest that rises or falls as the venture's success is measured.

The biggest problem in the impact investment world right now is the idea of measuring impact. It's easy to track growth in a typical start-up; how is it scaling? How much money has it made? But with impact investing, how do you measure the good you're doing in the world? It's subjective and quite difficult to measure. Tools, such as the Impact Reporting and Investment Standards (IRIS) and the Global Impact Investing Rating System (GIIRS), have been developed to assist investors in evaluating impact, but it's far from an exact science.

Beware the Mission Drift

One reason for caution when raising investment capital is "mission drift" over time. Mirjam Schöning says this is a major challenge social entrepreneurs face.

"Most so-called social or impact investors coming in are looking for returns of more than 10 percent. How much social impact can you generate with those expectations?" she says. "That leads to a slow mission drift of the organization. The social entrepreneur may be more social mission-oriented, but as you get a board, the perception is that you're running an expanding business, and it can lead to a detrimental effect on the people they're trying to help and benefit."

In other words, the desire to please investors may cause an entrepreneur to veer from his or her social goal or relax the policies of the business in order to concentrate on income generation. For instance, a business whose mission is to provide affordable housing to low-income citizens might begin to target more middle-class customers in order to collect higher profits. This causes customer distrust, which, ironically, affects the bottom line negatively. Waiting for the right investor rather than accepting the first money offered can be key to avoiding this problem.

Be aware of mission drift, whether it's profit/investor related, accidental or the company starts to move in another direction. If the company chooses to change directions, make sure to look at the mission statement too, so that you stay in alignment. Have your mission connect to the heart of what you do, that emotion connects customers easier to the company.

One thing we've also learned about our mission, is that if we stay in alignment with our mission, the money will come.

Resources

- **Social Capital Markets (SOCAP):** "At the intersection of money and meaning" is the tagline for this annual series of events designed to connect global innovators with investors, foundations, and institutions that could provide funding assistance. Through its newsletter and various articles in a variety of media, SOCAP communicates the latest news about this sector.

- **Good Capital:** An investment firm with a venture capital fund that targets social enterprises. In addition to speeding the flow of capital, Good Capital is "committed to collaborating with peers, contributing thought leadership, sharing our experiences, and creating innovative products and processes that enables the market for socially minded capital to flourish" (from website).

- **Global Impact Investing Network (GIIN):** A not-for-profit organization committed to improving the effectiveness of impact investing by addressing its barriers, including measurement of social impact and education of investors themselves about the social enterprise sector.

The Rise of the B Corp

The Benefit Corporation is an interesting development worth explaining. We have asked Rich Dad Advisor Garrett Sutton, the author of *Start Your Own Corporation* and *Run Your Own Corporation*, among other Rich Dad Advisor books, for his take on this trend.

An interesting side note: As a young attorney in Washington, D.C. in the early 1980s, Garrett worked for Bill Drayton and Ashoka in its formation stages. Here are Garrett's thoughts:

When Ben & Jerry's, the socially active ice cream maker, was put up for sale in 2000, the company faced a challenge, both internally and externally: To whom could it sell, and to whom did it owe a duty in the sale?

The company received two offers. One came from a socially minded purchaser with values that were closely aligned to those of Ben and Jerry's. The other came in from the huge multinational corporation Unilever, the makers of, among numerous other brands, Slim-Fast, Lipton Tea, Dove, Axe, Vaseline, VO5 shampoo, and Hellman's Mayonnaise.

The Unilever offer was at a higher price. But the lower offer was a better fit in terms of the company's existing culture and mission. They had a real dilemma on their hands. The choice was up to Ben & Jerry's board of directors. Their corporate attorneys advised them that by accepting the lower offer, they could be sued by the shareholders. The board was reminded that to maximize shareholder value and to uphold their fiduciary duties to their investors, they had to accept the highest bid.

Technically, this was the correct counsel. Numerous court cases have upheld the requirement that directors do what's best for the shareholders. (See eBay Domestic Holdings, Inc. v. Newmark 16A.3d1 (Del. Ch. 2010), a Delaware case holding that corporate directors are obligated to maximize shareholder value.)

And so Ben & Jerry's was sold to Unilever.

But the issue of whom the company must benefit—the shareholders, or other groups and interests—was raised once again. The business judgment rule protects directors who act in good faith and with loyalty to the company. Loyalty to others causes a loss of that protection, as Ben & Jerry's directors were keenly aware.

At the same time, a growing number of entrepreneurs and investors seeking to remedy environmental and social problems had begun to form. There was a percolation of ideas on how best to do this. A key issue for many of these forerunners was how to solve problems in a business context, without worrying about generating the highest profit. Profits, yes. The business had to be sustainable or else no one would benefit. Otherwise, there was no point to it. But maximum profits? No, there had to be a way to be profitable without worrying whether you'd left a dime or a dollar on the table, without worrying you'd be sued for failing to maximize shareholder value.

A nonprofit group known as B Lab took up the cause. Their position was this: If you could tweak the traditional model a bit, perhaps you could change the whole business dynamic. Perhaps problems could be efficiently solved in ways never before imagined.

And that's what is now happening.

But before we look into the new Benefit Corporation, let's explore why its primary alternative never really worked in this environment.

The not-for-profit (or nonprofit) corporation is familiar to most. Upon obtaining a 501(c)(3) designation (named after the applicable IRS code section), certain tax benefits are granted. Contributions by supporters are tax-deductible. Any monies raised by the nonprofit are tax-exempt. So a 501(c)(3) charity that raises $10,000 from each of its ten donors won't pay taxes on the $100,000 raised, and the ten donors will each get a tax deduction on that $10,000 contribution. A nonprofit that pursues a clearly defined charitable purpose and follows all the rules will be fine.

But there are certain restrictions that limit the usefulness of nonprofit corporations. First, they can't distribute their profits, which makes it impossible to attract investors.

You will never hear someone say: "You can't believe the dividends I'm raking in from Ronald McDonald House!" It simply doesn't work that way. As a contributor to a 501(c)(3) nonprofit corporation, your dividends are spiritual (doing good) and practical (reducing your income tax bill), but they are not actual (cash back).

Additionally, in spite of the United Way scandal pertaining to misuse of funds, nonprofits must limit the amounts they pay their employees. Thus, it's much harder for nonprofits to bring in, benefit, and keep talented people. Social Capitalists seeking to solve big hairy problems will need the best and the brightest, and they are going to have to pay them. The need for world-class human capital makes nonprofits unsuited for the big challenge.

Finally, the nonprofit rules limit activities that generate revenue. Sustainable and expanding operations that are the norm in the private sector are severely restricted by the federal tax laws in the nonprofit realm.

So the need to attract investors, pay talented people, and grow a business, along with the need to benefit groups other than exclusively shareholders, led to the creation of the Benefit Corporation.

Benefit corporations are traditional corporations (featuring limited liability protections and the same taxation) with three additional changes. Benefit Corporations must have:

1. A corporate purpose to positively impact society and the environment

2. An expanded fiduciary duty to consider the interests of workers, communities, and environments (as well as shareholders)

3. An annual report describing the company's overall social and environmental performance

B Lab managed to get the Benefit Corporation ball rolling in Maryland, which first authorized its use in 2010. A handful of other jurisdictions have followed, including California and New York. Legislation is pending in even more states, and we can expect Benefit Corporations to spread to all 50 states, much like LLCs did in the 80s and 90s. Plus, since 2005, the laws in Britain have similarly allowed for "community interest companies." Comparable legislation is now being considered in other countries as well.

B Lab also has a certification process for companies that voluntarily meet a high standard of social and environmental performance. It is known as the Certified B Corporation. One does not have to be a Benefit Corporation to be a Certified B Corporation, and vice versa. And know that there is confusion afoot: Both Benefit Corporations and Certified B Corporations are commonly known as B corps. (Note: From here on, we will refer to Benefit Corporations as B corps.)

Several key B corp issues will get to be worked out in the coming years. Will investors take to B corps? The movement toward socially responsible investing is certainly impressive. Over \$2 trillion, or nearly 10 percent of all U.S. assets under management, are committed to socially responsible investments. Will investors be willing to receive lower returns for a greater good? Time will tell.

The stated purpose of a Benefit Corporation must be to create a "general public benefit." B corps are also allowed to identify one or more specific public benefit as their purposes. Section 102(a) of Model Legislation (a template for states to follow when drafting their B corp law) allows for a number of specific public benefits:

1. Providing low-income or underserved individuals or communities with beneficial products or services

2. Promoting economic opportunity for individuals or communities beyond the creation of jobs in the ordinary course of business

3. Preserving the environment

4. Improving human health

5. Promoting the arts, sciences, or advancement of knowledge

6. Increasing the flow of capital to entities with a public benefit purpose

7. The accomplishment of any other particular benefit for society or the environment

The idea is that by combining a general and specific public benefit, the corporation is protected from answering solely to the financial interests of various stakeholders. But how far does that protection extend? Do B corps have an 80 percent duty to shareholders? A 51% duty? Or do they have zero responsibility to shareholders? Since the law is so new, we don't yet know. To be safe, we suggest that you always remember the investors (and their money) who brought you to the dance. Again, this is why selecting the right investor from the start, one whose involvement won't later lead to mission drift, is crucial.

Similarly, the directors of a B corp must review a number of issues when considering what is best for the company. Section 301(a)(1) of the Model Legislation requires that directors:

> *shall* consider the effects of any action or inaction upon: (i) the shareholders of the benefit corporation, (ii) the employees and workforce of the benefit corporation, its subsidiaries and its suppliers, (iii) the interest of customers as beneficiaries of the general public benefit or specific public benefit purposes of the benefit corporation, (iv) community and societal factors, including those of each community in which offices or facilities of the benefit corporation, its subsidiaries and its suppliers are located, (v) the local and global environment, (vi) the short-term and long-term interests of the benefit corporation, including any benefits that may accrue to the benefit corporation from its long-term plans and the possibility that these interests may be best served by the continued independence of the benefit corporation and (vii) the ability of the benefit corporation to accomplish its general benefit purpose and any specific public benefit purpose.

That is a lot to consider. How did you weigh all of them to arrive at the right decision? You can be sure that some directors will miss the old days when all they had to do was maximize shareholder value. That was easy. Now they have to factor in the workforce, the community, the environment, the purposes, and more. And in what order? By what percentage? What if you benefit the environment to the detriment of your workers? Can someone sue over too low a weighting being given to one issue on the board's decision? The old one-dimensional business judgment rule just became a three-dimensional societal matrix.

Again, with any new legal development, there will be unknowns. As with the duty to shareholders, the directors' requirement to consider all factors will be fleshed out and refined by court cases and future legislation. Our system can certainly deal with it, as it always has.

But the bottom line is that B corps will be a powerful and transformational force in business and society. As their uses spread, and as entrepreneurs tackle new challenges in new ways, you will see a swarm of B corps working for the good of the hive.

Thank you Garrett! We have become interested in the rise of the B Corp that we are proud to announce JHC became a Certified B Corporation during this writing! See - http://bcorporation.net/journeycenters

---

Chapter Thought

If you design your social enterprise around the *Rich Dad* B/I Triangle, investors will find your business more professional and attractive. Investors are looking for a great team, social value, and a positive cash flow. Address all three in your business plan, and be specific.

Chapter Eight

Companies with Conscience

"The moment for a new conception of capitalism is now; society's needs are large and growing, while customers, employees, and a new generation of young people are asking business to step up."

—Michael E. Porter and Mark R. Kramer, "Creating Shared Value"

It's important for us to say that you don't have to quit your job and start a social enterprise in order to do work that benefits the world or fights a social problem. You can be a Social Capitalist without being a social entrepreneur. After all, the emotional roller coaster and high risk of entrepreneurship is not for everyone. It's possible to turn a desire for social good into profit without starting a business with this sole intent. Many people love uniting with others and working for the missions of existing businesses, and are very good at it. We each have our own strengths, and we ought to play to them.

In fact, the most knowledgeable practitioners working today in the conscious capitalism space say that mobilizing existing businesses for good is where real world change will come from.

Why not be a social "intrapreneur"—someone who works from within companies or organizations to develop solutions to problems? Social intrapreneurs utilize what's right there in front of them—a team, financial resources, perhaps even a recognizable brand or name—to bring cause-oriented projects to life as insiders, relying on skills like teamwork and political savvy to get the job done.

"One thing people don't immediately think about is the benefit employees get out of social ventures, even though they don't run the companies. A lot of people want to do some good for the world, but need to make a salary," says Xavier Helgesen. "I think nonprofits, for a while, had the market cornered on that. A lot of corporate execs have left six-figure salaries to do it. But one of the unfair advantages a company with a social mission has is that they have access to employees that other companies don't have access to. And people like me won't ever work for a company that doesn't have good values. So companies will have to think about how they'll address that."

Fortunately, a growing number of businesses out there do realize that employees and consumers increasingly prefer businesses that have socially responsible practices. They also increasingly realize that those practices can actually enhance their productivity, contribute to producing better, more desirable products and services, and increase their bottom line.

The Wall

Increasingly, businesses are looking for ways to collaborate with NGOs and nonprofit organizations, or what Ashoka calls "the citizen sector," in order to leverage capitalism for societal good.

Like we've said before, words matter. As Ashoka explains on its website, "a growing number of sister organizations have sworn off the 'non-' words. Instead we use 'citizen sector' and 'citizen organization.' Why? Because citizens—people who care and take action to serve others and cause needed change—are the essence of the sector. We believe that when one or several people get together to cause positive social change, they instantly become citizens in the fullest sense of the word."

Bill Drayton discussed the importance of business collaboration with citizen-sector organizations (or CSOs) in his 2009 article "A New Alliance for Global Change" for the *Harvard Business Review*. "Collaboration between corporations and CSOs has reached a tipping point: It is becoming standard operating procedure," Drayton writes. "Indeed, we believe that if you're not thinking about such collaboration, you'll soon be guilty of strategy malpractice."

Drayton calls the current interest in social enterprises (business and social gain) a cyclical fashion, something that will go as quickly as it came. "People talking about social enterprise are intuiting something, but they're looking at it in the conventional way. We're in the middle of a fashion wave. They come every four to seven years. Investors see this seemingly new thing happening, and who wouldn't want to invest in something where you make money and you're doing good? You can point to examples of this throughout time. However, the newly discovered idea becomes 'hot' and 'in,' and then many good people come in with money. But the number of opportunities doesn't suddenly multiply. Eventually, many of the funds dry up because they can't find the deals. Business/social collaborations are both important and growing, but these episodic in and out tides of investors do not help."

Social entrepreneurs change things at the systemic level, but it's as if there's a wall between CSOs and businesses that has traditionally prevented the two from working together effectively. So it's been the work of social entrepreneurs that has truly torn down walls.

Take, for example, Muhammad Yunus. Numerous CSOs have been deployed throughout Bangladesh and the rest of the developing world for decades to work directly with the impoverished and hungry. Meanwhile, banking institutions, with their primary responsibility being to stakeholders, have traditionally shied away from loaning to the poor, considering their lack of collateral or income too risky. There was a wall between business and society that Grameen Bank effectively eradicated.

That's not to say that businesses don't care about people—they very often do. Many of them take part in corporate philanthropy.

Corporate philanthropy has a long and rich history in which American companies were founded on the idea that it was their responsibility to give back. In doing so, they would champion causes like United Way or the local symphony through sponsorships, table purchases at fundraising dinners, or through employee-raised donations.

Corporate philanthropy, then, is a bit like business sending an envoy over the wall to support society.

But progressive companies go beyond that, into CSR, where they have actual touch points with society.

CSR, or corporate social responsibility, is a term that refers to initiatives that account for business' impact on society or the environment. Going beyond philanthropy, CSR programs sustain business while protecting and improving the lives of societies touched by the business. It's as if businesses engaged in CSR are cutting holes into the wall.

One of the most lauded examples of CSR in action is that of Rommel Juan and his business, Binalot Fiesta Foods.

Binalot is a globally recognized leader in shared value through its CSR program, DAHON. Begun in 2007, DAHON (*Dangal At Hanapbuhay para sa Nayon*) begins with the humble banana leaf, which is what Binalot's Filipino-style fast foods are wrapped in ("Binalot" means "wrapped" in Filipino) to lock in their flavor. DAHON helps farmers from Nagcarlan, Laguna, which is about 100 kilometers south of Manila, by facilitating the purchase of banana leaves.

The community is Binalot's dedicated supplier and cutter of the leaves; the relationship not only benefits Binalot by providing a quality, safe, reliable supply of leaves, but it benefits the community. The women who cut the leaves now earn roughly 200 pesos each day, and farmers are assured of a steady supply of customers (and thereby income). Meanwhile, leaf trimmings, which used to be tossed into trash heaps, are now used as compost materials in the community.

Binalot even provided a much-needed renovation and new coat of paint to the community's chapel/day care center. Binalot is currently exploring the possibility of vegetable gardens, to increase the supplies that farmers can provide to the restaurant.

The DAHON program became reality after Typhoon Milenyo hit the Philippines in 2006, wiping out the banana leaf crops in Luzon, which had always been the source of Binalot's leaves. "Then we had to import banana leaves from other islands, and it was expensive," remembers Juan, who started the business with his brother and based its products packaging on their mom's method of preparing their food for picnics, wrapping food in banana leaves for easy portability.

"We couldn't price it that way for our franchisees, so we absorbed the cost," he continues.

It was an unsustainable practice that would soon have driven Binalot into the ground had Juan's aunt, who had run her own chain of coffee shops, not taken Juan to a forum about corporate social responsibility in Indonesia. "I realized we could help people and it would be good for our business as well. Because of the typhoon, we went straight for the community in Laguna, where most of the banana leaves come from."

He had expected the idea to be wildly embraced by the community, but that wasn't the case. It took a few attempts to convince farmers of the idea that they believed might be constructed to take advantage of their already vulnerable state. Instead, they only wanted Rommel to take their kids back to Manila and give them jobs.

But Juan was sure his idea would work, if only he could get buy-in. Finally, a community leader stepped up and agreed to organize the community and satisfy Binalot's first order for banana leaves: one bundle, which could provide enough leaves for about 200 dishes served at Binalot.

"So then we ordered 300 bundles," says Juan. "He was happy and shocked when we were back the next week. I had to explain to him that it was an ongoing thing!"

Because of the CSR, Binalot was assured it could conduct its business with a steady, reliable, high-quality supply of banana leaves. And the lives of the people of Nagcarlan have been improved as a result.

The program became a huge success right out of the gate. In 2007, UPS awarded Binalot Fiesta Foods with the centennial prize for its "Out-of-the-Box" small business competition—a $10,000 award that went right back to the community of Laguna, working with its women to streamline the leaf-cutting operation and employ them at a fair rate of pay.

The awards kept coming: the 2008 Anvil Award of Merit from the Public Relations Society of the Philippines, recognition from

Entrepreneur Magazine's 2009 Franchise Awards as Best Local Homegrown Franchise and Fastest-Growing Franchise, and recognition from the Philippine Retailers Association as one of the Outstanding Filipino Retailers. In 2010, Binalot took home a $20,000 Intel-AIM Corporate Social Responsibility award.

"There's a saying that if you give, it comes back to you a thousand-fold. For us it came back twenty-thousand-fold," says Rommel.

He says that two things really helped make the DAHON program successful, and he advises that others embracing a CSR consider them:

1. "Somebody should be in charge, because otherwise it goes away because nobody takes care of it." He explains that Binalot has a CSR manager who provides updates at every meeting, and it's integral to any strategic company discussion.

2. In the case of working with a developing village or country, Juan suggests getting local government or community leaders involved. "I think it helped that the head of our community became the captain of this project. Look for someone like that, someone to be your partner at the local level to organize and take ownership of it."

Another company that has embraced corporate philanthropy that extends to CSR is Julie Smolyansky's Lifeway Foods. Lifeway not only uses natural, organic ingredients sourced by sustainable local farms in its kefir, but it utilizes renewable energy in its carbon neutral manufacturing plant.

"I came back [from Bangladesh] feeling frustrated that women and children—especially girls—suffer incredible poverty, and I felt I had some role in helping," Julie says.

But she felt disenchanted with traditional fundraising, which she describes as "buy a table at a dinner, hear a speaker, get a little inspired, pay hundreds of dollars for a table or $5000 for a silent auction item, and it becomes more of a networking opportunity than working on the ground, making real change."

Through her experiences with Every Mother Counts, she's seen firsthand the impact of microfinance loans from such sources as Grameen Bank, and how a loan of just $5-$15 might allow a woman to purchase a chicken, or a sewing machine, in order to start a small business. "I think the micro-finance model allows its participants to take ownership and be accountable for the loan funds." It teaches them to fish, she says. Lifeway intends to employ this concept on its own, and will offer small loans to girls and women that would enable them to start kefir-production operations in their villages. At the time of this writing, the company is currently in the site-selection process, and the first Lifeway Village should be underway within a year.

"For us, this program is part of our mission to empower people to make better decisions about their health," Smolyansky says. "This is an extension of that. It's not a strategy for us, it's the core of who we are. I wouldn't outsource this, and it's not a trend to jump into. This is how we've always been as a company."

However, corporate social responsibility is what is most frequently understood by today's companies to be an expression of collaboration with the citizen sector, and in some companies, that has had unexpected consequences. One danger of CSR is that it becomes a portfolio point for the company, something that shows they're giving and that makes them look good to customers. In many cases, CSR programs became very small portions of the business, off to the side and not usually acknowledged as part of the business, and they become the home of controversies and stakeholder complaints. Rather than focusing on helping communities, for a lot of folks in CSR programs, their jobs mostly involve addressing issues raised by advocacy or boycotting groups. And a lot of CSR has ended up that way.

Gradually, however, companies have begun to acknowledge the wall, and are not only striving to get through it, but are seeking ways to tear it down. So instead of giving money or even giving a hand up to poor villages by bringing them into the supply chain, smart companies realize that they should invest in what they know and can make a difference in, where it aligns with their business.

These opportunities are what Michael Porter and Mark Kramer, the founders of Foundation Strategy Group (FSG), a nonprofit social impact consulting firm, call "shared value," or what Drayton refers to as the hybrid value chain model (HVC). FSG's concept of "shared value" is at the intersection of business and society—it's the complete alignment of the interests of business, consumers, and the planet at large.

Michael Porter and Mark Kramer wrote an article for the *Harvard Business Review* entitled, "Creating Shared Value," in which the concept is explained in this way: "[M]ost companies remain in the 'social responsibility' mind-set in which social issues are at the periphery, not the core. The solution lies in the principle of shared value, which involves creating economic value in a way that *also* creates value for society by addressing its needs and challenges."

With the shared value, or HVC model, collaborations between corporations and citizen-sector organizations provide increased benefits, increased strength, and wins for all parties involved. "When you tear down this wall between business and society, systemically, the way entrepreneurs do, and you look at a wall that cuts across the world, you take that down and you're creating millions of jobs."

He points to the housing industry as an example. In fall of 2010, the Indian government was reporting that roughly 24.7 million affordable homes were required to meet the demand of the legions of people without homes. Meanwhile, roughly two-thirds of its labor force is comprised of "informal workers," who do such work as selling vegetables at the local market. Their wages, while often providing for their families, go undocumented, making it impossible for them to qualify for financing on even small, affordable homes through traditional avenues.

Banks won't finance them, and builders won't build homes without capital markets to pay for them. The citizen-sector organizations, which work with the residents on the ground and understand their needs and ability intimately, are not skilled at real estate development or construction, nor can they get business to act.

What they have is a wall—one that prevents the sides from working together. "You can't solve this problem unless you get the strength of business to do what it's good at, and get the citizen sector to do what it's good at. Then it works," says Drayton.

With guidance from Ashoka and its Fellows, business and CSOs work together on an HVC called Housing For All India, which was created to tear down that wall.

Research supported by Ashoka and conducted by CSOs demonstrated to developers in India that there was a real demand for low-income housing at the $15,000 USD level, and they could finally see that they would turn a profit building it. Meanwhile, Ashoka Fellows are working with banks to develop financing products for informal workers by demonstrating similar research about these workers' incomes, to show proof that banks will benefit from this emerging market.

"Builders build, and they're happy to do more of it. They love this new market," says Drayton. "Financers have a big new market now, too. The citizen sector has a new way to serve its clients and have a revenue stream that means they don't have to work with the government, which they hate. And people there can now get homes ... If you translate 24.7 million homes at $15,000 each, that's a $400 billion market failure that we can now serve. And every one of those transactions is a hybrid (business/social) value chain. Our goal is that five to six years from now, anybody in any sector, when they think about their strategy for growth, will have as one of their first questions, 'Is there a wall anywhere near us?' If there is, they will know that they very probably have a major productivity, and therefore wealth and service, breakthrough within reach—as long as they know how to build a hybrid value chain, bringing the best parts of the previously divided groups together in intelligent collaboration."

There are almost always walls or obstacles along the way. It's being able to recognize them, finding a solution or knowing who to go to in finding a solution in order to move forward. The world is full of entrepreneurs and people who want to make a difference, and when we can collaborate, we can move a lot faster towards a solution.

To identify similar walls that could become opportunities, companies are increasingly turning to organizations like Foundation Strategy Group (FSG), TechnoServe and Hershey Cause for guidance in developing partnerships with NGOs, nonprofits, governments, foundations, or causes that align with their missions, and communicating them to the world. Even the Schwab Foundation is developing an exchange between CEOs to strengthen and embed conscious capitalism into their corporate strategies.

"Initially, our clients were corporate, and it was about getting the highest profile clients," explains Chris Hershey. "But over the five to ten years of doing that work, I realized the work we loved was when it was helping people. It was more fulfilling to help foster kids, to get shoes on people, etcetera, than to sell Pepsi. We carved out a specialty in projects for good, that make a contribution." Hershey Cause has on its roster of present and past clients such companies as Kaiser Permanente, Dr. Pepper, Lawry's Foods, Allergan, Columbia Pictures, Disney, Sony, Bank of America, and Wells Fargo – all of whom have some social responsibility, shared value, or philanthropic effort built into their businesses.

TechnoServe acts as a catalyst and broker, in that it identifies businesses in developing countries that are struggling, and harnesses resources from such partners as Coca-Cola, Cargill, Nestle, and The Bill & Melinda Gates Foundation to provide financial assistance to businesses in developing countries while nonprofit TechnoServe channels its energies into business support.

For instance, TechnoServe, working with Coca-Cola and the Gates Foundation, launched a corporate social responsibility partnership in 2010 that put more than 50,000 small fruit farmers in Uganda and Kenya into the supply chain for Coca-Cola's drink production. Money infused into the partnership through TechnoServe has been intended to help increase the farmers' productivity and double their incomes by 2014, by making them suppliers for the fruit drinks sold by Coca-Cola in those countries.

According to a press release distributed by TechnoServe about the collaboration, Nathan Kalumbu, Coca Cola's East & Central Africa business unit president, said, "This partnership is a great example of sustainability. By partnering with tens of thousands of local farmers, we can help increase their incomes while meeting our needs for locally sourced fruit, benefiting both the community and our business."

What FSG does is work with funders—corporations and foundations, primarily—to develop partnerships that enable them to channel funds into projects that have social or environment impact.

Take for example, its former client, the Mars Corporation, a $30 billion candy maker, and its Cocoa Sustainability Strategy.

In the chocolate business, there's one thing that can't be replaced, and that's cocoa. It makes chocolate chocolate, and there's no replacement for it. It's grown by small farmers in just four countries—Cote d'Ivoire, Ghana, Nigeria, and Cameroon, though Indonesia plays a minor role. But, essentially, those four countries produce about 70 percent of the world's chocolate; Cote d'Ivoire produces most of the world's cocoa.

Cocoa grows on trees, and as those trees approach about 20 years in age, they become less productive. In Cote d'Ivoire some trees are 35 or 40 years old. But there are roughly a million small-holder cocoa farmers whose survival relies on cocoa. They are poor, have small landholdings, are unable to improve or replace their trees, have no access to fertilizers or pesticides, and have no way to update their agricultural knowledge. Meanwhile, Cote d'Ivoire has difficult conditions in terms of corruption and taxation policies.

Mars, Inc., one the worlds leading chocolate companies, relies on this supply of cocoa, and needed to step in because the quality of that supply was in question. So Mars made a real investment in a Cocoa Sustainability Strategy, and with FSGs help in consulting with CSOs, the World Bank, the local government, and agricultural experts, Mars took a shared risk in the production of cocoa. Conditions for cocoa production and exports were improved and streamlined, and as a result, the quality and quantity of the cocoa Mars, and eventually other chocolate companies, received were consistently high.

In essence, what FSG does is work with companies on how they can use their power, resources, and know-to make investments in social issues in which they have a stake. Then FSG consults on how to involve governments, foundations, or other agencies or organizations to secure assistance and advocacy.

So the key seems to be not simply doing well as a company for the sake of doing good. Alignment with the capitalistic mission of the company—satisfying stakeholders—is not only okay in this business model, but it is absolutely key to the success of both the advancement of the social cause and of the company itself. They share the risk, and the reward.

Making Social Responsibility Part of Your Business

Beware of simply hopping on the bandwagon, though. Any effort at a CSR or shared value proposition should be authentic, and not simply a way to pander to consumers. "It's a hot button for me, one of those things a lot of us in the space are concerned about," Chris Hershey says. "We (at Hershey Cause) encourage business to do this, but ideally it's done with authenticity and strategy. You see a lot of green-washing, and companies chasing [causes] that they think will make them look good, like if fast food comes out in support of an anti-obesity campaign ... Do the things that complement your core business and interests. I'd encourage folks to think about it rigorously—how does it support your brand, is there a brand fit, does it make sense? We've seen strange, cobbled-together efforts where a lot of money has been spent but it doesn't pass the 'sniff test.'"

Rommel Juan suggests that any effort at corporate capitalism should come "from the top and cascade down, and be shared by everybody."

Many employees have a skillset to do the job they were hired for. To further have them be connected to the mission, social responsibility or cause the company is in alignment with strengthens the brand, the company, the staff and ultimately the customers and consumers.

Julie Smolyansky echoes this sentiment. Her father's natural desire to take care of others was the premise on which Lifeway was founded, and that played a big role in her commitment to CSR. "It's natural when you grow that way, to continue offering a helping hand. And if it starts at the top, it trickles down."

Where to Start With Your Business

When Blake Mycoskie befriended Argentinian children while traveling, and discovered that many of them didn't have shoes—a protective measure against disease and infection and a requirement at many schools in that area—he developed TOMS Shoes (which Blake says refers to "tomorrow") and the one-for-one business model. All it took to send a pair of shoes to someone in the world who needed it was for a customer to buy a great new, fashionable, competitively priced pair from the TOMS Shoes website (www.toms.com) today, and a new pair would be sent to that needy person tomorrow. Given the choice between any other pair of shoes purchased online at a comparable price and a TOMS pair, customers could double the reward for the same amount of money.

The same goes for buying Annie's Homemade macaroni and cheese, supporting locally sourced, sustainably produced, organic products, and buying, for instance, Kraft mac and cheese. Or, for that matter, buying a book from Better World Books instead of Amazon. A book is a book is a book. If we're not paying any more than we would otherwise, why not also support a great cause in the process, right?

In fact, consumers are twice as likely to buy or recommend a product associated with a cause they care about.

So here's the point: Companies like these and many others are going to continue making a dent in revenues generated by large corporations that don't have such socially responsible missions. With consumers having high expectations for businesses to have responsible policies (if not a role in a hybrid value chain), along with historically low confidence in Corporate America, and increasing desires among employees to work with companies with conscience, you can't afford not to build social responsibility into your business model.

This doesn't have to mean completely changing your business. Even small businesses can start with:

- Building sustainable practices into your operations—using solar energy or locally produced materials, for instance

- Making charitable giving a standard practice, in a way that's tied to your business' mission

- Ensuring that your employees are treated with dignity and respect.

For instance, Rommel Juan says that Binalot continues seeking ways to support other communities, including promotion of biodegradable packaging to other fast food companies, and the use of electric bicycles for food deliveries instead of cars. And Lifeway Foods uses renewable energy in its manufacturing facility.

But here's the key: You have to talk about it. "If we're in a consumer society, we vote with our dollars," says Julie Smolyansky. "I feel like it's a marketing strategy to tell the story of what we're doing. Plenty of companies do this, and they don't share it. Customers will support those businesses that align with their interests and do good for the world, if they have the choice."

Chapter Thought

Whether you are an employee or the owner of a business, look at what you can do now to start, enhance, or get involved in a social cause. Knowing your "why" can start you on this path. Does it align with the company's values? Is there a current organization you can partner with to serve this cause?

Our "why" is healing families who are coping with addiction; that is our social cause. We are profitable, and we give away thousands of dollars in scholarships for treatment, and we donate money, time and resources to other social causes in the community. We feel a social responsibility to better this world in many ways. The world is crying out for change. Are you willing to take a stand and make a difference?

Chapter Nine

Building a Business That Makes Sense: The Social Capitalist's Blueprint

"If ideas are to take root and spread, therefore, they need champions—obsessive people who have the skill, motivation, energy, and bullheadedness to do whatever is necessary to move them forward: to persuade, inspire, seduce, cajole, enlighten, touch hearts, alleviate fears, shift perceptions, articulate meanings and artfully maneuver them through systems."

—David Bornstein, *How to Change the World*

It's often thought—by people who struggle with the concept of entrepreneurship—that people who go out and start businesses have been gifted with rare intellect and courage. It's believed that entrepreneurs were either blessed with a certain kind of academic genius, or have received special training that enables them to turn ideas (which we all have) into viable enterprises.

But as you've seen through our experiences, none of this was true.

In fact, we would venture to say that the traits entrepreneurs possess have nothing to do with schooling or IQ, or even having grown up in a family in which entrepreneurship was encouraged. The traits are persistence, internal drive, and willingness to take risks. These traits build emotional intelligence, which assists you in coping with the ups and downs of the business cycle.

Some might argue that it's foolhardiness that keeps people like us from coming back, repeatedly, with the same idea and working to bring it to fruition despite a chorus of people warning us against it. But we believe that the one thing that distinguished us from other people we knew, worked with, or had grown up with was our particular brand of bulldog-like stubbornness.

We so stubbornly believed that we had a better way of doing things than what was already being done, that our experiences uniquely qualified us and predestined us for this work, and that we were worthy of receiving capital to get our idea off the ground, that we clasped our jaws tightly onto it and refused to let go, even when everyone else told us to forget it and go home. We could clearly see the vision that others could not. We kept waving it in front of people's faces until *finally* they heard what we had to say and gave us a chance.

In his year-long journey of exploration meeting citizen-sector leaders and social entrepreneurs in preparation for starting his nonprofit Prepared 4 Life, Michael Holthouse got the opportunity to discover exactly what made successful entrepreneurs tick, and his findings mirror ours.

"One of the big things I learned is that there are really two kinds of learning. When most Americans think of education, they immediately jump to school—reading, writing, and math, the great equalizers. But when you do the research and see the studies, academic success has almost no correlation to life success. There's some, but hardly any. It's the second side of education that bears all the impact. It goes by different names, but it's largely social and emotional skills. The ability to have a vision for your future, set goals, communicate well, work well with others. It's the integration of ideas and hard work, and discipline, and sacrifice for long-term benefit. It's all this stuff that our families are supposed to teach us. But because of the breakdown of the family in America, most people don't learn them. It's those skills, those life skills that separate really successful people from unsuccessful people.

Being passionate and committed to building the business is another strong trait. Having that strong "why" is another factor in the stubbornness that keeps us and many other entrepreneurs going.

"What's so interesting, at least to me, is that if you go to Google and type in 'characteristics of an entrepreneur,' what you'll find out is that great entrepreneurs are masters of these social and emotional skills, not necessarily masters of academic skills. Some are, but it's not the academics that are the breakthrough for them. It's about being loyal, trustworthy, managing life by values, communicating, imparting ideas... So entrepreneurship is at the very basis of really important stuff, the first being that it's how you build life success, and the second being that it's the basis of America, capitalism, free enterprise, and what makes us the leaders in the world."

Jon Carson, a serial entrepreneur and the co-founder of BiddingforGood.com, says while many people can be entrepreneurs, not *everybody* can. He also sees persistence among the distinct character traits found in entrepreneurs. Others on his list include good listening skills, the grit to stay with it through the ups and downs, being a good judge of people in order to build good teams, and being good salespeople. "To sell anyone, from the key employee hires to the first customers or the investors, on your idea, you need to be good at sales."

Note that we haven't distinguished here between social entrepreneurs and any other business entrepreneur, and the reason is that the two aren't all that different. While social entrepreneurship is unique in that it seeks social change as its primary goal, the capitalistic desire to earn a living is contingent upon the basic fundamentals of business.

As we've said, Social Capitalists don't necessarily have to be entrepreneurs. Whether working from the inside as intrapreneurs, leading a corporate social responsibility or shared value effort through an existing business, or starting your own new business, you can be a Social Capitalist if your for-profit work creates positive social change.

But we are business owners firmly rooted in such *Rich Dad Series* concepts as the B/I Triangle and passive income generation, which have been essential keys to our triple-bottom line of profit, social value, and freedom. And we feel that an entrepreneurial approach has enabled us to do the most good.

We've done quite a bit of research through our experiences in building Journey Healing Centers and in creating this book, and we've been able to distill a blueprint for social entrepreneurship.

We've found that the "secret sauce" of Social Capitalism really has just five basic ingredients:

Ingredient #1: A feasible solution to a proven problem

As Kreece Fuchs puts it, "If you're building it as a business, you need a product customers are going to want. That's true of any business, and it's not to be ignored."

It sounds terribly basic, but in their quest to make a social impact, a lot of social entrepreneurs overlook it. Kreece's mentor, David Murphy, says that way too many social entrepreneurs lead with their hearts instead of their heads.

"This doesn't differ one iota from entrepreneurship in general, in that if the marketplace is picking the winners and losers, you need to subject your ideas to all the rigors of it. It's a great business idea that solves a problem for the customer, and you've thought through how you're going to be sustainable," says Murphy.

We opened the first Journey Healing Center in 2002, having concluded through research that rates of addiction were skyrocketing. Since then, rates of substance abuse have gone even higher, and we've added locations to meet that demand. In just the three years from 2007 to 2010, the number of marijuana users in the U.S. increased by 3 million, and between 2006 and 2010, the number of antidepressant prescriptions increased by 21 million.

Meanwhile, the National Institute on Drug Abuse says that although approximately 23.5 million people in the U.S. needed treatment for substance abuse in 2009, only 2.6 million of them received it. Among that 2.6 million, only about half of them actually completed their programs.

At Journey Healing Centers, we've found that a family-centered approach that focuses on achieving life balance and providing free, lifetime after-care, we've managed to see a completion rate of about 95 percent, which far surpasses national statistics.

In other words, we found a unique and feasible solution to a proven problem, and after nearly a year of hard work and overcoming obstacles, we created a product that our guests—our "customers"—wanted.

Throughout this book, we've introduced you to Social Capitalists around the world who have done the same thing. Wanting to do something good for society or the planet is absolutely a worthy goal, but that's not enough of a foundation for you to assume people will buy from you.

In Mirjam Schöning's list of the 7 steps of successful entrepreneurship, which we referred to in Chapter 2, she says "Study approaches that lead to the same impact you are trying to achieve. Is your approach really as unique as you think it is? Are there more proven methods to achieve the same outcome from which you can learn?"

She adds that this seems to go against the grain of the typical social entrepreneur, who often becomes so single-mindedly focused on solving a problem that he or she may forget to consider what's being done about it in the world already.

"Few really take the time to look at the competitive landscape," Schöning says. "We are always rather shocked at how little the candidates to the Schwab network seem to know about similar approaches of other organizations."

Chapter Thought

Regardless of your social mission, be sure to do a thorough market analysis before establishing any new enterprise.

Ingredient #2: A powerful mission, or "why"

Why do you want to start your enterprise? What's driving you? Did a transformative experience in your life guide you to this point? Three such experiences did that for Lisa and me: my near-death experiences as a result of alcohol abuse, Lisa's taking a stand for herself (resulting in my positive experience in rehab, where I met our mentor and guide in this industry, Chris Spencer), and my dad's gift of *You Can Choose to Be Rich.*

When those three events came together for us, the vision for our future became crystal clear, and there was nothing else in the world we would ever consider doing once that vision had been established. Our early experiences with the 24-hour hotline—the tearful calls of pain and, later, gratitude—showed us that we were, and still are, absolutely on the right path.

The partying lifestyle that had been ingrained in us, one that throughout our lives had been glossed over as glamorous and fun, clearly had the potential to injure or kill, and I had been part of the problem as a nightclub employee. But all at once, we could no longer sit by and let it go on; we had to become part of the solution.

In his book about social entrepreneurs, *How to Change the World*, David Bornstein tells of an opportunity he had to listen to Bill Drayton as he briefed Ashoka's Fellowship candidates in Rio de Janeiro about the selection criteria. In that speech, Drayton told candidates, "Entrepreneurs have in their heads the vision of how society will be different when their idea is at work, and they can't stop until that idea is not only at work in one place, but is at work across the whole society ... An entrepreneur is not happy solving a problem in one village or two schools."

So until you are possessed by an idea, driven to plow forward in answer to your "why," it is unlikely that you'll create any kind of change.

And when you've identified your mission, focus wholly on that. Be careful of mission drift in order to please customers, employees, or investors, and don't allow a desire for profit to override your mission. Kreece Fuchs experienced this in the early days of Better World Books. The inventory system he and Xavier had created to manage their stock had proven so useful and user-friendly that they considered licensing the software. "It ended up being a distraction, and didn't do either company justice," says Kreece.

> It comes down to building a business that makes sense. One that solves a social problem and does good for humanity. Money is the by-product; it is the reward for being in service and seeking to elevate and empower those around you.

Profit is the 90-degree angle, the result of having a mission-driven, socially conscious enterprise.

In the end, the impact of a social enterprise must primarily be social, and the entrepreneur must, as Bill Drayton says, seek systemic change. Veering from that will ultimately do everyone, including those being served, a disservice. Your mission is everything.

Chapter Thought

Ask yourself this question, and be completely honest with yourself: If you did nothing about the problem, whatever problem is bothering you, could you live with it? Because if you couldn't, you've found your "why," and you likely have the makings of a social entrepreneur.

Ingredient #3: A winning team

We learned very early on that, while it made sense to be generalists who understood at least the basics of all facets of our business, it was crucial to play to our strengths. Building policy and procedure manuals, counseling, cooking for guests ... these things aren't our strengths. Our strengths lie in applying the principles of business and management that we've spent years studying. That's why we hired a team of people who possess those other unique strengths.

But as we've also learned the hard way, when we faced the threat of no licensure, that it's not enough to hire people based on their experiences or likeability, or because they were our friends or they made great promises. We also required a team that was as committed to our mission as we were, and who possessed the necessary business skills—integrity, professionalism, attention to detail, and knowledge in their subject area—that meant they could get the job done.

It turns out that a social enterprise's team is one of the clearest indicators of its success. David Murphy, who has judged business plan competitions and now serves as Associate Dean of Entrepreneurship at Notre Dame, says that one of the things he looks at first to determine the viability of a social enterprise is its team.

"For any kind of entrepreneurship, you need a heck of a team," he says. "And really, in the social entrepreneurship world, you need people who share your passion to change the world for the better.

But here's where I see social entrepreneurs being less rigorous about the talent they need around them. They've got their heads in the clouds, and that translates into how they hire people and put teams together. They say, 'Oh, my roommate sat up at night with me for two years and talked about clean drinking water in Haiti. He gets it, we're brothers.' But he's not what you need, really, if you're going to scale. So they get soft on the talent part ... You have to be rigorous and thoughtful about the team or you doom your chances."

In building a team it's good to look at three things: 1. Their skill set for the position, do they meet the requirements for the specific job description. 2. Are they a cultural fit, do they fit into the company culture. 3. Relationships, what are their relationship skills and what is their network, can they build outside relationships that align with the business.

Jon Carson believes so strongly in the power of a good team that he has spent years honing his interviewing techniques to specifically draw the right people, and significant investment is made in hiring for any position to ensure the right fit of talent and mission alignment. He says his biggest mistake throughout his years as an entrepreneur was making bad hiring decisions.

He says that now, at BiddingforGood.com, the people in charge of hiring all ask different questions, to ensure that they're painting the most well-rounded picture of the applicants. He rarely trusts references, he says, because that usually doesn't provide an accurate picture of how each applicant will do in the new position, with the existing culture and team.

"Also, we never hire a senior-level person without a deep psychological testing profile," Carson adds, explaining that an external third-party interviewer conducts several hours' worth of testing.

Related to teams, another big challenge that Mirjam Schöning sees in social enterprises is what she calls "founder's syndrome," which is hesitance to relinquish control.

"In most businesses, you have boards and investors, mechanisms that overrule the founder when it's in the interests of the company or organization," she explains. "That's often lacking in social enterprises. It's difficult to scale beyond a certain point because they may not see the need to empower other people in the organization. More managerial people are needed to come in provide structure and processes to a growing social enterprise. The founder is the charismatic visionary, the person who gets the door opened, but they're seldom the managers you need in order to see them grow. In the Schwab network, I have seen very few entrepreneurs who would claim to be visionaries and good managers at the same time, and they're also among the most successful. The entrepreneurs who are successful from the get-go recognize their strengths but have managers who run the day-to-day operations and processes."

In our particular experience with Journey Healing Centers, we found ourselves working with professionals who specialized—namely doctors and counselors. We found that self-employed "S" specialists don't wear multiple hats well; rarely do they know the essentials of building a business, which is really where we excelled. Having some specialists on your team is important, but a few generalists are essential in bridging the gaps.

Never underestimate the importance of the make-up of your team—it can mean the difference between success and failure.

Chapter Thought

When interviewing a potential employee, create an environment that puts the candidate under pressure, so that you can see who he/she really is. At Journey Healing Centers, one tool we use is the *Cashflow 101* game. We have brought in four candidates at a time and played the game with them. You'll learn a lot about a person when playing the game in the environment, as games are reflections of our behavior. Depending on the position to be filled, we look at different games or techniques that will enable us to see people for who they are.

Ingredient #4: A fundamentally sound business model

Kreece Fuchs, Xavier Helgesen, David Murphy and many other practitioners and academics in the world of social enterprise all say that having the goods baked right into the business model is intrinsic to success.

"I think one mistake I've seen a lot is people confusing a cause with a good business model," says Xavier. "So I've seen people come up with something that seems like a wonderful thing to do for the world but isn't all that interesting as a business, and they'll try to brand it as a social enterprise. One company I know of was trying to source products in Africa, to benefit those people economically, and sell them through e-commerce. But from Senegal the shipping for a small item was about $50, which makes it unfeasible. That's the real challenge. It's far easier to start with the economic opportunity you've identified, and make sure the business is engineered to target your cause, rather than, 'My social goal is X,' and then trying to make the business model fit."

Better World Books has been hailed as a prime example of a business model that works, precisely because it does exactly this—

capitalizes on people's normal buying habits (buying books online) by turning that purchase into a benefit for society. TOMS Shoes, Grameen Bank, and dozens of others bear out this truth.

"In Better World Books, what we're going to do to change the world is so absolutely tied to the business," says David Murphy. "Say Amazon bought it out and it went public; would we change the model? The reality is, we wouldn't, because the minute we no longer get our books for free through donations, it collapses. A lot of social entrepreneurs have a business idea that contributes part of the profits to charity, and that's nice, but it's not embedded deeply into the business model. What they're solving is peripheral to the business. I look for it buried into the model."

So, in fact, do impact investors like Good Capital. Founding Principal Kevin Jones wrote, in an article for Social Capital Markets, about the $2 million investment Good Capital made in Better World Books. He wrote, "Social enterprises where the mission drives the margin can grow faster than those that have to focus on two bottom lines, where the cost of doing good has a negative impact on profit margins."

Key to establishing a business model that spells success is drafting a thorough, comprehensive business plan. Again, this is no different from starting any business, even when a social mission is in play.

All the experts we spoke with said that the real measure of success, even when an enterprise is social in nature, is still the business plan—its execution and the entrepreneurs' commitment to it. There's no way around it. Our funding, as we've said, was contingent upon it, and it took several drafts, mistakes, and follow-through to get it our plan right.

TechnoServe's Business Plan Competition (BPC) Study for 2009 evaluates the benefits that the competitions, offered to entrepreneurs in developing countries in a variety of businesses, gave to the participants. The practice of creating a business plan for competition gave participants a significant edge, whether they won awards or not. Participants:

- Generated twice the one-year sales growth and 2.5 times the two-year sales growth as non-participants

- Created nearly 2.5 times more jobs over two years

- Mobilized nearly three times as much capital

- Were 1.5 times more likely to follow through on their plans to start or expand their businesses, and then much more likely to formalize them

- Were nearly twice as likely, as new businesses, to survive two years

The study reported, "In focus groups, we learned that the BPC emphasis on creating a business plan was of great value, forcing entrepreneurs to explore and resolve key issues." Although not all business plans were devised for social enterprises in the BPCs, some were, and the results were no different for those with social missions.

David Murphy says that when social entrepreneurs fail to secure start-up capital, it's not usually a case of funds not being available; it's usually due to a failure to pass the business plan "sniff test":

"Does the plan address the fundamental questions? What problem does it solve? What's the distribution strategy, or sales plan? Who's involved? It seems obvious, but it's amazing how many people tell me how great their product is, and I ask, 'Who's the customer? How will you sell the product? Who's the sales channel? Will you crowd-source it?' They just look at me with a blank stare. Then they'll say, 'I'll build a website. I'll build it and they'll come.' They're naïve about generating revenue. Naturally, any investor will say, 'I don't care how great your aspiration to change the world is, this plan stinks.' People in the social entrepreneurship space are naïve about business models; they have the idea that they're changing the world, and they think, 'Who wouldn't want to buy from me?' I'm not disputing that a lack of capital is a hindrance, but I've seen plenty of good deals that would have no trouble getting funded. It all comes down to the business model, the team, all the things that help not just social entrepreneurs, but entrepreneurs in general."

Note that this is what the B/I Triangle is all about: Too many people get caught up in the product. While product is important, everything else in the B/I Triangle supports the product, and not the other way around.

Mirjam Schöning also recommends that, in creating your business model, that you plan to generate revenue from day one, and that you build evaluation and measurement into your processes from the beginning, in order to show proof of impact. This can be beneficial as you seek capital for growth and expansion.

In terms of scaling the business, as Mirjam Schöning argues, a social franchise is perhaps the best way to expand into other locations or countries. "What we arguably need most today are entrepreneurial people that take up a brilliant model from one part of the world and implement and adapt it in another."

For this reason, Grameen Bank is now in approximately 100 countries.

This is why Journey Healing Centers are in six locations in two states. Each one meets a unique demand, for both the range of guests we accommodate and the states in which we're located. Our 10-year business plan says that we will be operating in nine countries with 12 healing centers, which serve more than 5,000 guests per year. With the extremely high demand and our measurable goal, we know where we are today and where we're going. Journey Healing Centers will have global healing programs that can reach people with addiction problems worldwide.

Michael Holthouse points out that Lemonade Day was established as a sort of franchise that individual communities can customize and operate themselves. This was purposeful. "In 501(c)(3) organizations and social enterprises, where we're driving to solve the world's problems is that we've got to figure out how to allow more people to take the credit so they can invest in this thing more deeply. I think that's really how you have significant growth," he says. "We provide the best practices, the tools, the methodologies, the processes, the products, the branding, and they're the ones that breathe life into Lemonade Day in each city ... So what we do is figure out a way where local communities can mold Lemonade Day to have the greatest impact in their communities, and *they're* the heroes. We're in the background, and we want to see them succeed."

Chapter Thought

If you're serious, really serious, about a social venture of any sort, demonstrate this by taking the time to draft a really comprehensive business plan. Carefully consider your business model to ensure that the social mission is integral to the profit generation, not on the periphery.

Ingredient #5: Personal Development

As we've been saying, we committed individually to ourselves and to each other early on to personal development, to continually educate ourselves in the *Rich Dad* principles of growing wealth, and in the many aspects of the addiction treatment business. We know that we're never going to be too old or too successful to learn, and we truly believe that this has been integral to our success. As a matter of fact, we study more now than we ever did in school. Our learning will never stop, and we're studying subjects that interest us, which have tremendously positive effects on our lives and the lives of others.

We always look at how we can implement training into our lives, and the lives of our families, teams, businesses and guests. No matter the course or subject, we are determined to take something valuable away from it that we can put to use.

If there's something we must know, we don't say, "I don't know," or "I can't do that yet." We say, "Let's learn how we can do it." And then we spend the time it takes to learn it. Every time we have done that, it has paid off for us in terms of smoothing out challenges in the business, working with our guests, addressing our relations with our employees and colleagues, building our business, and increasing our triple-bottom line.

We learned the lesson about personal development from the best.

Shortly after closing on our original Utah property, having just received our start-up capital from Arvis, he announced that he wanted to come see his investment for himself. We were quite proud of the progress we had made and the responsible way we had handled his money, so we were, of course, happy to have him come see it.

We picked him up from the Salt Lake City airport, and in the car on the way back to the property, we decided this was a good opportunity to get to know Arvis and absorb the wisdom he had gained in his years as a businessman. We asked him how he got started. "I always watched my money and what I spent my money on. And I'm cautious about it," he said.

I remember after finishing school having the thought of being happy I was done learning. Little did I know that my learning was just beginning. School didn't teach about the real world experiences I was going to have, it gave a lot of content for certain subjects but real world experience, personal development and how to build a business was hands on. Life is about learning, becoming who we are, finding our purpose and going for it. It's about learning from our mistakes, taking the good, the bad, the ugly and the great and doing something positive with it.

I thought about our earliest meetings with him—the plastic chair coverings, the debate with a waiter over the market price for fish.

At first, I had seen his frugality as odd, even something to chuckle over. But now, a new business owner, I took comfort from his response. Lisa and I had already begun taking that step. It was reassuring to know that someone as successful as Arvis could have started in such a simple way. Not to say that we are as frugal as he is, but we continue our journey in financial education so that we can make smart financial decisions and create financial freedom in order to live a rich life.

What he said next, I will never forget. "How I got started was by going to a seminar. I did what they told us to do, and it worked, so I kept on doing it."

A seminar? Really? This was a huge affirmation for us. Having recently embraced the *Rich Dad* teachings and become almost religious in our studies of them, we had been teased by our friends, who called us seminar and book "junkies." They warned us that we were being ripped off, manipulated into spending money on useless products. And we'd come home with another $599 program and they'd tease us even more.

We had begun to learn that the people we surrounded ourselves with were no longer a support system that we could count on. They were stuck in a place we'd moved out of, and that was an important lesson. But even more important were the lessons we were learning everyday from our seminars and books, and we were thrilled by the ways in which we were growing and evolving every day because of the things we learned.

Through our work with addiction, we knew what a "junkie" really was. It's someone who will sacrifice everything to get what he or she wants, no matter what the personal cost or the cost to others. We knew we weren't "junkies." We were two people who had survived the darkness of addiction and were now committed to improving our lives and those of others. We were willing to invest our time, money, and resources in our future; many of our friends weren't. We actively applied the principles from the seminars and books to our lives and business. We looked for successful seminar teachers—not just successful on stage, but successful business owners off stage. We did what they told us to do and it worked, as Arvis said, so we kept doing it. It was that simple.

Arvis explained that he would buy property, use the extra cash flow to focus on one property at a time, and pay down the principle loan. Once that was paid off, he would then use extra cash to pay down the principle on the next property, and so on. This was compounding principle payments. It wasn't far off from what we learned from the *Rich Dad* books about how to pay off bad debt. Arvis' story and his success told us that we were on the right track.

This kind of learning may not be for everyone. Whether you learn from a seminar, a book, a professional networking organization, a class, or a volunteer duty, the point is, *never stop learning*. Business education is the difference between

Almost always we would come home with all these great ideas we learned and would want to implement, our friends would say, "Here they go again". Sometimes the ideas would work and sometimes not, but I knew that we would always attempt the new ideas because we would always learn something from it. Never be afraid to test a new idea, maybe only a part of it will take hold and be effective but always have the willingness to test something new. And be open to feedback, whether you like it or not, there could be another lesson or nugget in there.

being an individual or nonprofit with a cause and a Social Capitalist. Seek teachers and mentors. Be open to new ideas. Create open exchanges with others in your field or with similar roles as you. Find opportunities to have new experiences and learn something. Even negative experiences are teaching moments.

And always be willing to share what you know or have experienced with others. "One bit of advice to [social entrepreneurs] is to continue to work collectively ... to help establish and develop this 'field' of social entrepreneurship—this pragmatic idealism, however we might want to label it, that is encouraging innovative approaches," said J. Gregory Dees, Faculty Director at CASE, in that institution's publication, "The Past, Present, and Future of Social Entrepreneurship."

He continues, "I think they have to come together to have a common voice and to share issues and lessons with one another."

Kreece Fuchs, Chris Hershey and others recommend B Lab as a great organization, not only because of the access it provides to a supportive network, but because of the process for becoming a Certified B Corp, which steps a business through the rigors of becoming mission-focused, environmentally sustainable and responsible to both stakeholders and the world at large. "It's a great social network to be part of, which has been key," says Kreece. "I'd definitely encourage folks to reach out to other social enterprises for advice. It's practical, and there's a community of people who buy products from other social enterprises, so it's a community that's really been developing."

Chapter Thought

Congratulations for having taken this first step in your personal development by reading this book! We challenge you to join an organization, take a class, attend a seminar, sign up for coaching, or put together a book study group in the next month, in order to continue on your personal development path.

Chapter Ten

Final Thoughts

"Never depend upon institutions or government to solve any problem.
All social movements are founded by, guided by, motivated and seen
through by the passion of individuals."

—Margaret Mead

"Stay hungry. Stay foolish."

—*The Whole Earth Catalog*, May 1974

In sharing the story of our "Journey" with you, we've also spoken to
some of the major players in the Social Capitalism movement. From
that, we have learned a tremendous amount, and are exhilarated to realize
that we are only seeing the movement in its infancy.

We are, quite plainly, seeing the world change and become a better
place, largely because of Social Capitalists who are tearing down walls and
building bridges, from within companies and citizen-sector organizations,
or at the helms of brand-new ones.

A global community of people are putting their hands up instead of
putting their hands out, realizing that instead of criticizing governments
and corporations to fix things, they have the power to fix them themselves,
and that they can do so while also earning a profit.

Social Capitalists who fulfill a triple-bottom line:

- Are persistent self-starters

- Have a "why" propelling them to fight the status quo and
  fulfill a purpose

- Seek opportunities to learn
- Seek opportunities for the triple-bottom line: Profit, So-
  cial Value, and Freedom
- Seek mentors and colleagues with whom to exchange ideas
- Have an idea or solution to a problem
- Are possessed by that idea, and cannot rest until they
  achieve it
- Have a solid business plan
- Have a business model in which fulfilling the mission is
  inherently part of the for-profit activities of the business
- Have a winning team that aligns with the mission and
  business plan
- Look for opportunities to combine commercial business
  interests with citizen-sector concerns, putting capitalism
  to work for social good

There is no shame in being a for-profit social enterprise. We have always believed this, and our extensive research has proven us right.

"Sometimes still, there's a perception out there that says, 'the only way to do good in the world is the nonprofit model. If I'm nonprofit, people will know I'm not out for the money, and they can feel better about us,'" says David Murphy. "Sometimes, that's true. But if you're serious about pure social enterprise, and you're subject to the rigors of the marketplace, profit cannot be a dirty word. People have been conditioned to think it's evil. And I'm not disputing that there are dark sides of capitalism. We all know there are. But Grameen was set up as a for-profit, and there's a reason why it scaled; the profit gets reinvested. If you're going to build something with impact, you've got to be able to reinvest the profit, which means you've got to generate it."

But a strong social venture, he adds, is transparent. In that model, you're for-profit, you're proud of it, and you do good for people or the planet with that profit. "The two are not mutually exclusive."

And consider this: As Mirjam Schöning of the Schwab Foundation told Rahim Kanani of *The Huffington Post* in May 2011, "When we analyzed the entrepreneurs in our network over time, we noticed that the for-profit enterprises, or those with an earned revenue stream, grew, on average, three times faster than those purely focused on donations."

Over the years, some people have commented that we are "all about the money." We find this a bit ironic, because in fact we have never taken paychecks from the company. We provide a solution to a social cause and are committed to growing the company to serve more people; being for-profit enables us, as it does other companies, to expand more quickly, to provide a quality service, and work under fewer regulatory constraints in a free-market society.

So not only is capitalism compatible with a social mission, but it often results in a greater good for society as well as a more successful business.

Fred Kofman, author of *Conscious Business,* writes, "To be conscious means to be awake, mindful ... A conscious business fosters peace and happiness in the individual, respect and solidarity in the community, and mission accomplishment in the organization." In other words, be a conscious business means that we recognize what we do, how we do it, and what the effects of our actions are.

Capitalism is a socioeconomic system based on the principles of property rights, the rule of law, voluntary exchange, wealth creation, entrepreneurial initiative; in a capitalistic society, human activity and social organizations (businesses) reflect and embody these principles.

Additionally, remember to give it time. The Schwab Foundation won't consider businesses as candidates for its network that have been around for less than three years. You may not immediately reap huge financial benefits or even get out of the red for a while. Be patient. Nothing worth having came easily.

No Regrets

This book has been a lifetime in the making. In piecing together the story of how we moved from our earliest beginnings to where we are today, we've been forced to relive some of the darkest days of our lives, but we've also rejoiced in our most cherished moments. It's been an emotional journey for us, putting it all on paper. But through it all, we've learned one final truth: Our future lies within our past. By this we mean that our past is where we find all the clues to finding, living, and sharing our purpose. It's what led us to Journey Healing Centers and some of the happiest moments of our lives. And it's likely what will lead you to the next phase of your journey toward fulfilling your mission.

Like Steve Jobs said in his famous 2005 commencement speech at Stanford University, "You can't connect the dots looking forward; you can only connect them looking backwards. So you have to trust that the dots will somehow connect in your future. You have to trust in something—your gut, destiny, life, karma, whatever. This approach has never let me down, and it has made all the difference in my life."

It takes courage to find your purpose and live it, rather than settling for the predictability of a life that could also leave you hollow and unfulfilled.

Robert Kiyosaki's sister and a friend of ours, Tenzin Kacho, is a Buddhist nun ordained by His Holiness, the Dalai Lama. We traveled with the *Rich Dad* organization and Tenzin several years ago on a speaking tour in Sydney, Singapore, and Kuala Lumpur. Tenzin spoke of the three regrets people have at the end of life:

Failing to tell someone, "I love you."

Failing to forgive another.

Failing to take a leap of faith.

We want you to have no regrets today, tomorrow, or the next day. We want you to live the life you truly want and be free to give your gifts to the world. That's why we wrote this book. Take that leap of faith. Learn from all of it and know that you are great.

We look forward to our next book, in which we'll provide even more tips and advice on building a sustainable and successful business.

When times get tough—and they will—trust the process. Trust that when you connect the dots later, it will all make sense, and that each of those "dots" will have led you to where you were supposed to be.

Now, go out there and change the world!

About the Authors

Josh Lannon, CEO and Founder of Journey Healing Centers, has over 11 years experience in the behavioral health field. Journey Healing Centers currently has 6 owner-operated facilities under management in Utah and Arizona.

Josh is a Social Entrepreneur and has been the *Addiction Advisor* and *Social Entrepreneur* Advisor to the Rich Dad Organization since 2011. Josh is an inspirational leader and international speaker, who wanted to give back by building socially conscious enterprises after getting sober in 2001.

Josh and his wife Lisa co-authored the Rich Dad Advisor book *The Social Capitalist, Passion and Profits—An Entreprenurial Journey.*

Josh leads Journey Healing Centers with its headquarters located in Scottsdale, Arizona. JHC is an accredited private adult drug and alcohol program that has assisted thousands of individuals with successfully overcoming the power of addiction and reuniting with their families.

The recent mega trend of socially driven individuals and impact investors, using capital for a conscious cause has lead Josh and Lisa in creating Journey Healing Centers Franchise. JHC Franchise is changing the face of global drug and alcohol addiction treatment.

Josh has also dedicated the past 20 years to studying the martial arts. He has a "Professor of Arts" ranking as a 6th degree blackbelt as a personal student to the Grandmaster Mr. Paul Mills. Josh is a leading Professor at the AKKI annual international seminars and teaches karate seminars worldwide.

Current Affiliations:
Member of YPO (young presidents organization)
American Kenpo Karate Association - Board Member
Sales Partners Worldwide: Board Member
Journey Healing Centers Franchise – Founder
Rich Dad – Student and Advisor

Lisa Lannon, Co-Founder of Journey Healing Centers and Founder of Brooke Property Management, Lisa has over 11 years experience in the behavioral health field and managing property/investment portfolios.

Lisa's company Brooke Property Management oversees the luxury property portfolio to Journey Healing Centers around the world.

Lisa is a Social Entrepreneur and has been *Advisor* to the Rich Dad and Rich Woman Organization since 2010. She is an investor with a portfolio including residential real estate, apartment complexes, commercial buildings and oil & gas. Not to mention an incredible mom and international speaker.

Lisa supported her husband Josh getting sober and the couple decided to assist others get loved ones back by building Journey Healing Centers. She currently leads JHC's public relations campaigns featured in People Magazine, MTV, USA Today, Fox News and many others media outlets.

Prior to Journey Healing Centers, Lisa was a commissioned Law Enforcement Officer for the Las Vegas Nevada Police Department, where she was on the frontline to addiction and crime. Lisa was seen on the television show "Las Vegas Jails".

Lisa has been interviewed on Fox News, PBS, and PBS's Rich Woman, among many other media outlets and has written for the Rich Woman and Rich Dad Advisor's blog.

Current Affiliations:
Member of YPO

NotMYkid – Supporter

National Center for Missing & Exploited Children - Supporter

Make a Wish –Supporter

Rich Dad – Student and Advisor

References and Resources

Books and Information for Investors and Entrepreneurs
www.BZKPress.com
www.RDAPress.com
www.RichDadAdvisors.com

Social Capitalism
www.thesocialcapitalistbook.com
www.journeycenters.com
www.ashoka.org   www.betterworldbooks.com
www.hersheycause.com   www.lemonadeday.org
www.binalot.com   http://netimpact.org
www.technoserve.org   www.schwabfound.org
www.lifeway.net/LifewayWorld/CorporateSocialResponsibility.aspx
www.biddingforgood.com/auction/BiddingForGood.action

Real Estate
www.KenMcElroy.com
www.mccompanies.com

Asset Protection and LLC Formation
www.sutlaw.com
www.corporatedirect.com

Tax Planning
www.provisionwealth.com

Sales Strategies
www.salesdogs.com

The Rich Dad Company
www.RichDad.com

RICH DAD.™
ADVISORS

The Rich Dad Advisors series of books was created to deliver the how-to content to support Robert Kiyosaki's series of international bestsellers: *Rich Dad Poor Dad* and the Rich Dad series of books. In *Rich Dad Poor Dad*—the #1 Personal Finance Book of all Time—Robert presented the foundation for the Rich Dad principles and philosophies and set the stage for his context-changing messages that have changed the way the world thinks about money, business and investing.

The Rich Dad Advisors series of books has sold more than 2 million copies worldwide and BKZ Press, exclusive publisher of the Rich Dad Advisor series and the licensor of International Rights for the series, will be releasing several new titles that will expand both the scope and depth of the series.

Rich Dad Poor Dad represents the most successful book on personal finance in our generation. Over the last 15 years, its messages have inspired millions of people and impacted tens of millions of lives in over 100 countries around the world. The Rich Dad books have continued to international bestseller lists because their messages continue to resonate with readers of all ages. *Rich Dad Poor Dad* has succeeded in lifting the veil of confusion, fear, and frustration around money and replacing it with clarity, truth, and hope for every person who is willing to commit to the process of becoming financially educated.

In order to make good on the promise of financial literacy and ultimate freedom, Robert Kiyosaki assembled his own team of personal and trusted advisors, proven experts in their respective fields, to deliver the only complete 'how-to' series of books and programs that takes the messages of Rich Dad to the streets of the world and gives each reader the step-by-step processes to achieve wealth and income in business, investing, and entrepreneurship.

BZK Press is driven by several of Kiyosaki's actual Advisors who have committed to take the messages of Rich Dad, convert them to practical applications and make sure those processes are put in the hands of those who seek financial literacy and financial freedom around the world. The series gives practical, proven processes to succeed in the areas of finance, tax, entrepreneurship, investing, property, debt, sales, wealth management and both business and personal development. Three of these trusted and accomplished Advisors—Blair Singer, Garrett Sutton, and Ken McElroy—are the driving forces behind BZK Press.

BZK Press is proud to assume the role of publisher of the Rich Dad Advisor series and perpetuate a series of books that has sold millions of copies worldwide and, more importantly, supported tens of millions in their journey toward financial freedom.

Best-Selling Books
in the Rich Dad Advisors Series

by Blair Singer

SalesDogs
You Don't Have to Be an Attack Dog to Explode Your Income

Team Code of Honor
The Secrets of Champions in Business and in Life

by Garrett Sutton, Esq.

Start Your Own Corporation
Why the Rich Own their Own Companies and Everyone Else Works for Them

Writing Winning Business Plans
*How to Prepare a Business Plan that Investors will Want to Read —
and Invest In*

Buying and Selling a Business
How You Can Win in the Business Quadrant

The ABCs of Getting Out of Debt
Turn Bad Debt into Good Debt and Bad Credit into Good Credit

Run Your Own Corporation
*How to Legally Operate and Properly Maintain Your Company
into the Future*

The Loopholes of Real Estate
Secrets of Successful Real Estate Investing

by Ken McElroy

The ABCs of Real Estate Investing
The Secrets of Finding Hidden Profits Most Investors Miss

The ABCs of Property Management
What You Need to Know to Maximize Your Money Now

The Advanced Guide to Real Estate Investing
How to Identify the Hottest Markets and Secure the Best Deals

by Tom Wheelwright

Tax-Free Wealth
*How to Build Massive Wealth by **Permanently** Lowering Your Taxes*

by Andy Tanner

Stock Market Cash Flow
Four Pillars of Investing for Thriving in Today's Markets

by Josh and Lisa Lannon

The Social Capitalist
Passion and Profits
—An Entrepreneurial Journey

JOURNEY HEALING CENTERS

"Journey saved me from loosing my family and my life. Thank you." Rachel

Journey Healing Centers is a private adult drug and alcohol treatment program. JHC is not a government funded or a court ordered program. The JHC programs are typically self-funded by the guests themselves however, insurance reimbursement may apply depending on ones policy.

JHC is fully accredited by the JOINT Commission of Health Care and globally recognized. JHC has assisted thousands of people overcome the grips of addiction and reunite their families back together again.

JHC provides residential treatment, outpatient and sober living in luxurious properties. The ADA (American disability act) in the United States categorized addiction as a disability. Because of this, JHC is permitted to open healing centers in residential neighborhoods. JHC carefully selects its locations to assure privacy, amenities and destination locations. Their success rate is that 95% of the guests successfully complete the programs! This far exceeds industry standards.

JHC's inspiration comes from the alumni who have overcome the control of addiction. The alumni, family members and loved ones often share their amazing stories of experience, strength and hope. The words *"Thank you for giving me my loved one back"* is commonly heard at JHC.

JHC utilizes only the most effective therapeutic modalities to promote wellness, healing and self-discovery. Their unique blend of group therapy, lots of individual counseling, experiential education and holistic programming combine to offer a treatment experience second to none.

If you know of someone who could benefit from Journey Healing Centers services, please feel free to contact them on their 24-hour helpline. They are completely confidential and treat everyone with dignity and respect.

Get The Person You Love...Back

Private Drug & Alcohol Rehab

www.journeycenters.com

1-866-774-5119

JOURNEY HEALING CENTERS

Join the movement
JHC Franchise Opportunity

For over a decade Journey Healing Centers has successfully served thousands of everyday moms, dads, brothers, sisters, friends and professionals overcome the grips of addiction.

Our passion is to build socially conscious businesses that solve problems. Addiction is a rapidly growing problem in every culture, in every economic class and in tens of millions of households around the globe.

Sobering Statics

Alcohol abuse alone results in **2.5 million deaths each year**, more than those caused by AIDS and Tuberculosis.

Source: Geneva-based

There continues to be a large "treatment gap" in this country. In 2010, an estimated 23.1 million Americans (9.1 percent) needed treatment for a problem related to drugs or alcohol, but only about 2.6 million people (1 percent) received treatment.

Source: National Institute on Drug Abuse

"Based on the need in the market, the market for drug and alcohol treatment could reach $230 Billion. Even if only 1% seek **treatment it is a $2.3 Billion Market**."

Source: NIDA

A unique opportunity to make a difference

JHC Franchise is an accredited, proven system with years of experience in the field. JHC Franchise offers franchise systems for private adult drug and alcohol rehab from inpatient, outpatient to long-term sober living programs.

Our social cause is focused on "Getting the Person you Love...Back.

Our business is real estate.

Start the journey today for by joining a global franchise system that is solving a social problem; transforming lives and bringing families back together again.

Be the Change

If you are interested in learning more or joining the cause, please call 1-866-559-4203 or visit us at: www.journeycenters.com/franchise

Thank you for taking a stand with us.